ADHD Raising an Explosive Child

The Survival Guide for Kids with ADHD. A New Approach of Positive Parenting to Empower Complex Kids. Learn the Strategies to Help Your Children Self-Regulate

Mary Petersen

TABLE OF CONTENTS

Introduction

Attention deficit hyperactivity disorder (ADHD) is a neurodevelopmental disorder characterized by inattention, excessive activity, and impulsivity, otherwise not appropriate for a person's age. Some individuals with ADHD also display difficulty regulating emotions or problems with executive function. For a diagnosis, the symptoms should appear before a person is 12 years old, be present for more than six months, and cause problems in at least two settings (such as school, home, or recreational activities). In children, problems paying attention may result in poor school performance. Additionally, it is associated with other mental disorders and substance misuse. Although it causes impairment, particularly in modern society, many people with ADHD can have sustained attention for tasks they find interesting or rewarding (known as hyperfocus).

Despite being the most commonly studied and diagnosed mental disorder in children and adolescents, the precise cause or causes are unknown in most cases. Genetic factors are estimated to make up about 75% of the risk. Nicotine exposure during pregnancy may be an environmental risk. It does not appear to be related to the style of parenting or discipline. It affects about 5–7% of children diagnosed via the DSM-IV criteria and 1–2% when diagnosed via the ICD-10 criteria. As of 2019, it was estimated to affect 84.7 million people globally. Rates are similar between countries, and differences in rates depend mostly on how it is diagnosed. ADHD is diagnosed approximately two times more often in boys than in girls, although the disorder is often overlooked in girls because their symptoms are often less disruptive. About 30–50% of people diagnosed in childhood continue to have symptoms into adulthood, and between 2–5% of adults have the condition.

In adults, inner restlessness, rather than hyperactivity, may occur. Adults often develop coping skills which compensate for some or all of their impairments. The condition can be difficult to tell apart from other conditions and high activity levels within the range of normal behavior.

ADHD management recommendations vary by country and usually involve some combination of medications, counseling, and lifestyle changes. The British guideline emphasizes environmental modifications and education for individuals and carers about ADHD as the first response. If symptoms persist, then parent training, medication, or psychotherapy (especially cognitive behavioral therapy) can be recommended based on age. Canadian and American guidelines recommend medications and behavioral therapy together, except in preschool-aged children for whom the first-line treatment is behavioral therapy alone. For children and adolescents older than 5, treatment with stimulants is effective for at least 24 months; however, their long-term effectiveness is unclear, and there are potentially serious side effects.

The medical literature has described symptoms similar to those of ADHD since the 18th century. ADHD, its diagnosis, and its treatment have been considered controversial since the 1970s. The controversies have involved clinicians, teachers, policymakers, parents, and the media. Topics include ADHD's causes and the use of stimulant medications in its treatment. Most healthcare providers accept ADHD as a genuine disorder in children and adults, and the debate in the scientific community mainly centers on how it is diagnosed and treated. The condition was officially known as attention deficit disorder (ADD) from 1980 to 1987. It was known as a hyperkinetic reaction of childhood.

Chapter 1: Explanation of ADHD

ADHD is one of the most common neurodevelopmental disorders of childhood. It is usually first diagnosed in childhood and often lasts into adulthood. Children with ADHD may have trouble paying attention, controlling impulsive behaviors (may act without thinking about what the result will be), or be overly active.

ADHD is a mental health condition that can create challenges to a person's work, study, and home life. It usually appears during childhood. A person does not "grow out of" ADHD, but learning management strategies can help them enjoy a full life. Without treatment, which may include medication, a person may experience low self-esteem, depression, school problems, work, and relationships. Anyone who believes that a child may have ADHD should seek medical advice. Counselors, teachers, and other members of a child's support network can help them manage their symptoms and maximize their opportunities.

Attention deficit/hyperactivity disorder (ADHD) is one of the most common mental disorders affecting children. ADHD also affects many adults. Symptoms of ADHD include inattention (not being able to keep focus), hyperactivity (excess movement that is not fitting to the setting), and impulsivity (hasty acts that occur at the moment without thought). An estimated 8.4% of children and 2.5% of adults have ADHD.[1,2] ADHD is often first identified in school-aged children when disruption in the classroom or schoolwork problems. It can also affect adults. It is more common among boys than girls.

Symptoms And Diagnosis

It is normal for children to have trouble focusing and behaving at one time or another. However, children with ADHD do not just grow out of these behaviors. The symptoms continue, can be severe, and can cause difficulty at home or with friends.

A Child With ADHD Might:

- Daydream a lot
- Forget or lose things a lot
- Squirm or fidget
- Talk too much
- Make careless mistakes or take unnecessary risks
- Have a hard time resisting temptation
- Have trouble taking turns
- Have difficulty getting along with others

Many ADHD symptoms, such as high activity levels, difficulty remaining still for long periods, and limited attention spans, are common to young children in general. The difference in children with ADHD is that their hyperactivity and inattention are noticeably greater than expected for their age and cause distress and problems functioning at home, at school, or with friends.

ADHD is diagnosed as one of three types: inattentive type, hyperactive/impulsive type, or combined type. A diagnosis is based on the symptoms that have occurred over the past six months.

1. Inattentive Type: Six (or five for people over 17 years) of the following symptoms occur frequently:

- Doesn't pay close attention to details or makes careless mistakes in school or job tasks.
- Has problems staying focused on tasks or activities, such as lectures, conversations, or long reading.
- Does not seem to listen when spoken to (i.e., seems to be elsewhere).
- Does not follow through on instructions and doesn't complete schoolwork, chores, or job duties (may start tasks but quickly loses focus).
- Has problems organizing tasks and work (for instance, does not manage time well; has messy, disorganized work; misses deadlines).
- Avoids or dislikes tasks that require sustained mental effort, such as preparing reports and completing forms.

- Often loses things needed for tasks or daily life, such as school papers, books, keys, wallet, cell phone, and eyeglasses.
- Is easily distracted.
- Forgets daily tasks, such as doing chores and running errands. Older teens and adults may forget to return phone calls, pay bills and keep appointments.

2. Hyperactive/Impulsive Type: Six (or five for people over 17 years) of the following symptoms occur frequently:

- Fidgets with or taps hands or feet or squirms in seat.
- Not able to stay seated (in the classroom, workplace).
- Runs about or climbs where it is inappropriate.
- Unable to play or do leisure activities quietly.
- Always "on the go," as if driven by a motor.
- Talks too much.
- Blurts out an answer before a question has been finished (for instance, may finish people's sentences, can't wait to speak in conversations).
- Has difficulty waiting for his or her turn, such as while waiting in line.
- Interrupts or intrudes on others (for instance, cuts into conversations, games, or activities, or starts using other people's things without permission). Older teens and adults may take over what others are doing.

There is no lab test to diagnose ADHD. Diagnosis involves gathering information from parents, teachers, and others, filling out checklists, and having a medical evaluation (including vision and hearing screening) to rule out other medical problems. The symptoms are not the result of a person being defiant or hostile or unable to understand a task or instructions.

Besides, The Following Conditions Must Be Met:

- Several inattentive or hyperactive-impulsive symptoms were present before age 12 years.
- Several symptoms are present in two or more settings (such as at home, school, or work, with friends or relatives, in other activities).
- There is clear evidence that the symptoms interfere with or reduce the quality of social, school, or work functioning.
- The symptoms are not better explained by another mental disorder (such as a mood disorder, anxiety disorder, dissociative disorder, or a personality disorder). The symptoms do not happen only during schizophrenia or another psychotic disorder.
- Based on the types of symptoms, three kinds (presentations) of ADHD can occur:

3. Combined Presentation: If enough symptoms of both criteria inattention and hyperactivity-impulsivity were present for the past six months

Causes

While the exact cause of ADHD is not clear, research efforts continue. Factors that may involve developing ADHD include genetics, the environment, or problems with the central nervous system at key development moments. Scientists have not yet identified the specific causes of ADHD. There is evidence that genetics contribute to ADHD. For example, three out of four children with ADHD have a relative with the disorder. Other factors that may contribute to the development of ADHD include being born prematurely, brain injury, and the mother smoking, using alcohol, or having extreme stress during pregnancy.

Diagnosis

Deciding if a child has ADHD is a process with several steps. There is no single test to diagnose ADHD, and many other problems, like anxiety, depression, sleep problems, and certain types of learning disabilities, can have similar symptoms. One step of the process involves having a medical exam, including hearing and vision tests, to rule out other problems with symptoms like ADHD. Diagnosing ADHD usually includes a checklist for rating ADHD symptoms and taking a child's history from parents, teachers, and sometimes children.

Diagnosis In Children And Teenagers

Diagnosing ADHD in children depends on a set of strict criteria. To be diagnosed with ADHD, your child must have six or more inattentiveness symptoms or six or more symptoms of hyperactivity and impulsiveness. To be diagnosed with ADHD, your child must also have:

- Been displaying symptoms continuously for at least six months
- Started to show symptoms before the age of 12
- Been showing symptoms in at least two different settings – for example, at home, and at school, to rule out the possibility that the behavior is just a reaction to certain teachers or parental control
- Symptoms that make their lives considerably more difficult on a social, academic, or occupational level
- Symptoms that are not just part of a developmental disorder or difficult phase and are not better accounted for by another condition

Other Conditions That Resemble ADHD

Several medical conditions or their treatments may cause signs and symptoms similar to those of ADHD. Examples include:

- Learning or language problems
- Mood disorders such as depression or anxiety
- Seizure disorders
- Vision or hearing problems
- Autism spectrum disorder

- Medical problems or medications that affect thinking or behavior
- Sleep disorders
- Brain injury

Typical Developmental Behavior Vs. ADHD

Most healthy children are inattentive, hyperactive, or impulsive at one time or another. It's typical for preschoolers to have short attention spans and be unable to stick with one activity for long. Even in older children and teenagers, attention span often depends on the level of interest.

The same is true of hyperactivity. Young children are naturally energetic, they often are still full of energy long after they've worn their parents out. Besides, some children naturally have a higher activity level than others do. Children should never be classified as having ADHD just because they're different from their friends or siblings.

Children who have school problems but get along well at home or with friends are likely struggling with something other than ADHD. The same is true of hyperactive or inattentive children at home, but whose schoolwork and friendships remain unaffected.

When To See A Doctor

If you're concerned that your child shows signs of ADHD, see your pediatrician or family doctor. Your doctor may refer you to a specialist, such as a developmental-behavioral pediatrician, psychologist, psychiatrist, or pediatric neurologist. Still, it's important to have a medical evaluation first to check for other possible causes of your child's difficulties.

Risk Factors

Risk Factors For ADHD May Include:

- Blood relatives, such as a parent or sibling, with ADHD or another mental health disorder
- Exposure to environmental toxins such as lead, found mainly in paint and pipes in older buildings
- Maternal drug use, alcohol use, or smoking during pregnancy
- Premature birth
- Although sugar is a popular suspect in causing hyperactivity, there's no reliable proof of this. Many issues in childhood can lead to difficulty sustaining attention, but that's not the same as ADHD.

Complications

ADHD can make life difficult for children. Children with ADHD:

- Often struggle in the classroom, which can lead to academic failure and judgment by other children and adults

- Tend to have more accidents and injuries of all kinds than do children who don't have ADHD
- Tend to have poor self-esteem
- They are more likely to have trouble interacting with and being accepted by peers and adults
- Are at increased risk of alcohol and drug abuse and other delinquent behavior

Coexisting Conditions

ADHD doesn't cause other psychological or developmental problems. However, children with ADHD are more likely than others also to have conditions such as:

- Oppositional defiant disorder (ODD), generally defined as a pattern of negative, defiant, and hostile behavior toward authority figures
- Conduct disorder, marked by antisocial behavior such as stealing, fighting, destroying property, and harming people or animals
- Disruptive mood dysregulation disorder, characterized by irritability and problems tolerating frustration
- Learning disabilities, including problems with reading, writing, understanding, and communicating
- Substance use disorders, including drugs, alcohol, and smoking

- Anxiety disorders, which may cause overwhelming worry and nervousness and include obsessive-compulsive disorder (OCD)
- Mood disorders, including depression and bipolar disorder, which includes depression as well as manic behavior
- Autism spectrum disorder, a condition related to brain development that impacts how a person perceives and socializes with others
- Tic disorder or Tourette syndrome, disorders that involve repetitive movements or unwanted sounds (tics) that can't be easily controlled

Prevention

To help reduce your child's risk of ADHD:

- During pregnancy, avoid anything that could harm fetal development. For example, don't drink alcohol, use recreational drugs, or smoke cigarettes.
- Protect your child from exposure to pollutants and toxins, including cigarette smoke and lead paint.
- Limit screen time. Although still unproved, it may be prudent for children to avoid excessive exposure to TV and video games in the first five years of life.

Types

There are three different types of ADHD, depending on which types of symptoms are strongest in the individual:

1. Predominantly Inattentive Presentation: It is hard for the individual to organize or finish a task, pay attention to details, or follow instructions or conversations. The person is easily distracted or forgets details of daily routines.

2. Predominantly Hyperactive-Impulsive Presentation: The person fidgets and talks a lot. It is hard to sit still for long (e.g., for a meal or doing homework). Smaller children may run, jump or climb constantly. The individual feels restless and has trouble with impulsivity. Someone impulsive may interrupt others a lot, grab things from people, or speak at inappropriate times. It is hard for the person to wait their turn or listen to directions. A person with impulsiveness may have more accidents and injuries than others.

3. Combined Presentation: Symptoms of the above two types are equally present in the person. Because symptoms can change over time, the Presentation may change over time as well.

Scientists are studying cause(s) and risk factors to find better ways to manage and reduce their chances of having ADHD. The cause(s) and risk factors for ADHD are unknown, but current research shows that genetics plays an important role. Recent studies of twins link genes with ADHD. In addition to genetics, scientists are studying other possible causes and risk factors, including:

- Brain injury
- Exposure to environmental (e.g., lead) during pregnancy or at a young age
- Alcohol and tobacco use during pregnancy
- Premature delivery
- Low birth weight

Treatments

In most cases, ADHD is best treated with a combination of behavior therapy and medication. For preschool-aged children (4-5 years of age) with ADHD, behavior therapy, particularly training for parents, is recommended as the first treatment line before medication is tried. What works best can depend on the child and family. Good treatment plans will include close monitoring, follow-ups, and making changes, if needed, along the way.

Treatment for attention deficit hyperactivity disorder (ADHD) can help relieve the symptoms and make the condition much less of a problem in day-to-day life.

ADHD can be treated using medicine or therapy, but a combination of both is often best. Treatment is usually arranged by a specialist, such as a pediatrician or a psychiatrist, although a GP may monitor the condition.

Distinguishing Mood Disorders And ADHD

Inattention can occur in both ADHD and mood disorders. In ADHD, distraction is typically caused by external stimuli, whereas in mood disorders, the distraction is internal. Suspect a mood disorder or depression when the child displays:

- Irritability
- Depressed mood/sad (not always evident)
- Decreased interest in usual activities
- Appetite changes
- Unintended weight changes
- Sleep problems
- Changes in energy level, fatigue
- Feelings of worthlessness
- More difficulty concentrating
- Suicidal ideation or behavior

Diagnosis

Untreated mood disorders can make it harder to treat ADHD effectively, and it can be challenging to differentiate some behaviors seen in ADHD from those in mood disorders. When diagnosing mood disorders, consider the following types of questions:

- Family history

- Decreased involvement with friends or activities that are usually enjoyable for the child
- Changes in sleep (sleeping more or less)
- Decreased or dramatically increased energy level
- Threatened or actual self-harm or suicidal ideation
- Appetite changes
- Increased outbursts of temper
- Impact of symptoms on functioning

Medicine

There are five types of medicine licensed for the treatment of ADHD:

- Methylphenidate
- Lisdexamfetamine
- Dexamfetamine
- Atomoxetine
- Guanfacine

These medicines are not a permanent cure for ADHD but may help someone concentrate better, be less impulsive, feel calmer, and learn and practice new skills. Some medicines need to be taken every day, but some can be taken just on school days. Treatment breaks are occasionally recommended to assess whether the medicine is still needed.

If you were not diagnosed with ADHD until adulthood, a GP and specialist could discuss which medicines and therapies are suitable for you. If you or your child is prescribed one of these medicines, you'll probably be given small doses initially, which may gradually increase. You or your child will need to see a GP for regular check-ups to ensure the treatment is working effectively and check for signs of any side effects or problems.

It's important to let the GP know about any side effects and talk to them if you feel you need to stop or change treatment. Your specialist will discuss how long you should take your treatment, but, in many cases, treatment is continued for as long as it is helping.

1. Methylphenidate

Methylphenidate is the most commonly used medicine for ADHD. It belongs to a group of stimulants, which increase brain activity, particularly in areas that control attention and behavior.

Methylphenidate may be offered to adults, teenagers, and children over the age of 5 with ADHD. The medicine can be taken as either immediate-release tablets (small doses are taken 2 to 3 times a day) or as modified-release tablets (taken once a day in the morning, with the dose released throughout the day).

Common Side Effects Of Methylphenidate Include:

- A small increase in blood pressure and heart rate

- Loss of appetite, which can lead to weight loss or poor weight gain
- Trouble sleeping
- Headaches
- Stomach aches
- Mood swings

2. Lisdexamfetamine

Lisdexamfetamine is a medicine that stimulates certain parts of the brain. It improves concentration, helps focus attention, and reduces impulsive behavior. It may be offered to teenagers and children over the age of 5 with ADHD if at least six weeks of treatment with methylphenidate has not helped. Adults may be offered lisdexamfetamine as the first-choice medicine instead of methylphenidate. Lisdexamfetamine comes in capsule form, taken once a day.

Common Side Effects Of Lisdexamfetamine Include:

- Decreased appetite, which can lead to weight loss or poor weight gain
- Aggression
- Drowsiness
- Dizziness
- Headaches

- Diarrhea
- Nausea and vomiting

3. Dexamfetamine

Dexamfetamine is similar to lisdexamfetamine and works in the same way. It may be offered to adults, teenagers, and children over the age of 5 with ADHD. Dexamfetamine is usually taken as a tablet once or twice a day, although an oral solution is also available.

Common Side Effects Of Dexamfetamine Include:

- Decreased appetite
- Mood swings
- Agitation and aggression
- Dizziness
- Headaches
- Diarrhea
- Nausea and vomiting

4. Atomoxetine

Atomoxetine works differently from other ADHD medicines. It's a selective noradrenaline reuptake inhibitor (SNRI), which means it increases the amount of a chemical in the brain called noradrenaline. This chemical passes messages between brain cells, and increasing it can aid concentration and help control impulses.

Atomoxetine may be offered to adults, teenagers, and children over the age of 5 if it's impossible to use methylphenidate or lisdexamfetamine. It's also licensed for use in adults if symptoms of ADHD are confirmed. Atomoxetine comes in capsule form, usually taken once or twice a day.

Common Side Effects Of Atomoxetine Include:

- A small increase in blood pressure and heart rate
- Nausea and vomiting
- Stomach aches
- Trouble sleeping
- Dizziness
- Headaches
- Irritability

Atomoxetine has also been linked to some more serious side effects that are important to look out for, including suicidal thoughts and liver damage. If you or your child begins to feel depressed or suicidal while taking this medicine, speak to your doctor.

5. Guanfacine

Guanfacine acts on the part of the brain to improve attention, and it also reduces blood pressure. It may be offered to teenagers and children over the age of 5 if it's impossible to use methylphenidate or lisdexamfetamine. Guanfacine should not be offered to adults with ADHD. Guanfacine is usually taken as a tablet once a day, in the morning or evening.

Common Side Effects Of Guanfacine Include:

- Tiredness or fatigue
- Headache
- Abdominal pain
- Dry mouth
- Therapy

As well as taking medicine, different therapies can be useful in treating ADHD in children, teenagers, and adults. Therapy is also effective in treating additional problems, such as to conduct or anxiety disorders, that may appear with ADHD.

Some Of The Therapies That May Be Used Are Outlined Below.

1. Psychoeducation

Psychoeducation means you or your child will be encouraged to discuss ADHD and its effects. It can help children, teenagers, and adults make sense of being diagnosed with ADHD and help you cope and live with the condition.

2. Behavior Therapy

Behavior therapy provides support for carers of children with ADHD and may involve teachers as well as parents. Behavior therapy usually involves behavior management, which uses a system of rewards to encourage your child to control their ADHD. If your child has ADHD, you can identify the types of behavior you want to encourage, such as sitting at the table to eat. Your child is then given some sort of small reward for good behavior and has a privilege removed for poor behavior.

3. Parent Training And Education Programs

If your child has ADHD, specially tailored parent training and education programs can help you learn specific ways of talking to your child and playing and working with them to improve their attention and behavior. You may also be offered parent training before your child is formally diagnosed with ADHD.

These programs are usually arranged in groups of around 10 to 12 parents. A program usually consists of 10 to 16 meetings, lasting up to 2 hours each.

Being offered a parent training and education program does not mean you have been a bad parent, it aims to teach parents and carers about behavior management while increasing confidence in your ability to help your child and improve your relationship.

4. Social Skills Training

Social skills training involves your child taking part in role-play situations and teaching them how to behave in social situations by learning how their behavior affects others.

5. Cognitive-Behavioral Therapy (CBT)

CBT is a talking therapy that can help you manage your problems by changing the way you think and behave. A therapist would try to change how your child feels about a situation, potentially changing their behavior. CBT can be carried out with a therapist individually or in a group.

6. Other Possible Treatments

There are other ways of treating ADHD that some people with the condition find helpful, such as cutting out certain foods and taking supplements. However, there's no strong evidence of this work, and they should not be attempted without medical advice.

7. Diet

People with ADHD should eat a healthy, balanced diet. Do not cut out foods before seeking medical advice. Some people may notice a link between types of food and worsening ADHD symptoms. If this is the case, keep a diary of what you eat and drink and what behavior follows. Discuss this with your GP, who may refer you to a dietitian (a healthcare professional specializing in nutrition).

8. Supplements

Some studies have suggested that supplements of omega-3 and omega-6 fatty acids may be beneficial for people with ADHD, although the evidence supporting this is very limited. It's advisable to talk to your GP before using any supplements because some can react unpredictably with medicine or make it less effective.

Medication Treatments For ADHD - Mood Stabilizers (For ADHD With Mood And Behavior Problems)

Lithium, Carbamazepine (Tegretol and Valproic Acid (Depakote) have been used when mood disorders coexist with ADHD. One frequently sees bipolar patients with supposed comorbid ADHD or diagnosed solely with ADHD. This is becoming increasingly common in adults and kids thanks to the popularity of the ADHD diagnosis. The problem is that just about all bipolar patients have a disorder of attention. To differentiate between the two, it is sometimes helpful to look for symptoms that are seen in bipolar disorders but not usually in ADHD, for example:

- Racing thoughts
- Not needing to sleep or hypersomnia
- Changes in energy parallel to the above
- Tangential thinking
- Overspending, overcommitting
- Grandiosity
- Grandiose thrill-seeking (e.g., jumping off of high places)
- Psychosis.

When ADHD and Bipolar Disorder are comorbid, starting treatment with a stimulant in these patients will often exacerbate the hyperactivity, flatten effect, and greatly decrease appetite. Some doctors start instead with either clonidine or guanfacine plus one of the following mood stabilizers: lithium, carbamazepine, valproic acid, or lamotrigine.

Once the patient is stable on therapeutic doses, a stimulant can be added if ADHD symptoms remain; if necessary, an antidepressant is sometimes added.

The boundary between persistent hypomania and ADHD is unclear. The usual practice is to treat such cases with stimulants before puberty and with mood-stabilizing agents in adulthood.

Drug Monographs

Selected Medications Mentioned in this Section:

- Lithium Carbonate (Eskalith, Lithobisd, Lithonate, etc.)
- Divalproex Sodium / Sodium Valproate + Valproic Acid (Depakote)
- Carbamazepine (Tegretol)
- Lamotrigine (Lamictal)
- Guanfacine HCL (Tenex)
- Clonidine (Catapres)

Managing Symptoms: Staying Healthy

Being healthy is important for all children and can be especially important for children with ADHD. In addition to behavioral therapy and medication, having a healthy lifestyle can make it easier for your child to deal with ADHD symptoms. Here are some healthy behaviors that may help:

- Developing healthy eating habits such as eating plenty of fruits, vegetables, and whole grains and choosing lean protein sources
- Participating in daily physical activity based on age
- Limiting the amount of daily screen time from TVs, computers, phones, and other electronics
- Getting the recommended amount of sleep each night based on age

Identifying Symptoms Of ADHD

Signs of Attention Deficit Hyperactivity Disorder (ADHD).

1. Self-Focused Behavior

A common sign of ADHD is what looks like an inability to recognize other people's needs and desires. This can lead to the next two signs:

- Interrupting
- Trouble waiting their turn

2. Interrupting

Self-focused behavior may cause a child with ADHD to interrupt others while they're talking or butt into conversations or games they're not part of.

3. Trouble Waiting Their Turn

Kids with ADHD may have trouble waiting their turn during classroom activities or playing games with other children.

4. Emotional turmoil

A child with ADHD may have trouble keeping their emotions in check. They may have outbursts of anger at inappropriate times.

5. Fidgeting

Children with ADHD often can't sit still. They may try to get up and run around, fidget, or squirm in their chair when forced to sit.

6. Problems Playing quietly

Fidgetiness can make it difficult for kids with ADHD to play quietly or engage calmly in leisure activities.

7. Unfinished Tasks

A child with ADHD may show interest in lots of different things, but they may have problems finishing them. For example, they may start projects, chores, or homework but move on to the next thing that catches their interest before finishing.

8. Lack Of Focus

A child with ADHD may have trouble paying attention even when someone is speaking directly to them. They'll say they heard you, but they won't be able to repeat back what you just said.

9. Avoidance Of Tasks Needing Extended Mental Effort

This lack of focus can cause a child to avoid activities requiring sustained mental effort, such as paying attention in class or doing homework.

10. Mistakes

Children with ADHD may have trouble following instructions that require planning or executing a plan. These can then lead to careless mistakes, but it doesn't indicate laziness or a lack of intelligence.

11. Daydreaming

Children with ADHD aren't always raucous and loud. Another sign of ADHD is being quieter and less involved than other kids. A child with ADHD may stare into space, daydream, and ignore what's going on around them.

12. Trouble Getting Organized

A child with ADHD may have trouble keeping track of tasks and activities. This can cause school problems, as they can find it hard to prioritize homework, school projects, and other assignments.

13. Forgetfulness

Kids with ADHD may be forgetful in daily activities. They may forget to do chores or their homework. They may also lose things often, such as toys.

14. Symptoms In Multiple Settings

A child with ADHD will show symptoms of the condition in more than one setting. For instance, they may show a lack of focus both in school and at home.

Symptoms As Children Get Older

As children with ADHD get older, they'll often not have as much self-control as other children their age. This can make kids and adolescents with ADHD seem immature compared to their peers. Some daily tasks that adolescents with ADHD may have trouble with include:

- Focusing on schoolwork and assignments
- Reading social cues
- Compromising with peers
- Maintaining personal hygiene
- Helping out with chores at home
- Time management
- Driving safely

Looking Forward

All children are going to exhibit some of these behaviors at some point. Daydreaming, fidgeting, and persistent interruptions are all common behaviors in children. You should start thinking about the next steps if:

- Your child regularly displays signs of ADHD
- This behavior is affecting their success in school and leading to negative interactions with peers

ADHD is treatable. If your child is diagnosed with ADHD, review all of the treatment options. Then, set up a time to meet with a doctor or psychologist to determine the best course of action.

Symptoms Of Attention Deficit Hyperactivity Disorder (ADHD)

The symptoms of attention deficit hyperactivity disorder (ADHD) can be categorized into two types of behavioral problems:

- Inattentiveness
- Hyperactivity
- Impulsiveness.

Most people with ADHD have problems that fall into both these categories, but this is not always the case.

For example, some people with the condition may have inattentiveness problems but not with hyperactivity or impulsiveness.

This form of ADHD is also known as attention deficit disorder (ADD). ADD can sometimes go unnoticed because the symptoms may be less obvious.

Symptoms In Children And Teenagers

The symptoms of ADHD in children and teenagers are well defined, and they're usually noticeable before the age of 6. They occur in more than one situation, such as at home and school.

Inattentiveness

The main signs of inattentiveness are:

- Having a short attention span and being easily distracted
- Making careless mistakes, for example, in schoolwork
- Appearing forgetful or losing things
- Being unable to stick to tasks that are tedious or time-consuming
- Appearing to be unable to listen to or carry out instructions
- Constantly changing activity or task
- Having difficulty organizing tasks

Hyperactivity And Impulsiveness

The main signs of hyperactivity and impulsiveness are:

- Being unable to sit still, especially in calm or quiet surroundings
- Constantly fidgeting
- Being unable to concentrate on tasks
- Excessive physical movement
- Excessive talking
- Being unable to wait their turn
- Acting without thinking
- Interrupting conversations
- Little or no sense of danger

These symptoms can cause significant problems in a child's life, such as underachievement at school, poor social interaction with other children and adults, and discipline problems.

Related Conditions In Children And Teenagers With ADHD

Although not always the case, some children may also have signs of other problems or conditions alongside ADHD, such as:

1. **Anxiety Disorder:** Which causes your child to worry and be nervous much of the time; it may also cause physical symptoms, such as a rapid heartbeat, sweating, and dizziness

2. **Oppositional Defiant Disorder (ODD):** This is defined by negative and disruptive behavior, particularly towards authority figures, such as parents and teachers

3. **Conduct Disorder:** This often involves a tendency towards highly antisocial behavior, such as stealing, fighting, vandalism, and harming people or animals

4. **Depression**

5. **Sleep Problems:** Finding it difficult to get to sleep at night and having irregular sleeping patterns

6. **Autistic Spectrum Disorder (ASD):** This affects social interaction, communication, interests, and behavior

7. **Epilepsy:** A condition that affects the brain and causes repeated fits or seizures

8. **Tourette's Syndrome:** A condition of the nervous system characterized by a combination of involuntary noises and movements (tics)

9. **Learning Difficulties:** Such as dyslexia

Symptoms In Adults

In adults, the symptoms of ADHD are more difficult to define. This is largely due to a lack of research into adults with ADHD.

- ADHD is a developmental disorder, and it's believed it cannot develop in adults without it first appearing during childhood.
- But it's known that symptoms of ADHD often persist from childhood into a person's teenage years and then adulthood.
- Any additional problems or conditions experienced by children with ADHD, such as depression or dyslexia, may also continue into adulthood.
- By the age of 25, an estimated 15% of people diagnosed with ADHD as children still have a full range of symptoms, and 65% still have some symptoms that affect their daily lives.
- The symptoms in children and teenagers are sometimes also applied to adults with possible ADHD.
- But some specialists say how inattentiveness, hyperactivity, and impulsiveness affect adults can be very different from how they affect children.

For example, hyperactivity tends to decrease in adults, while inattentiveness tends to worsen as adult life pressures increase.

Adult symptoms of ADHD also tend to be far more subtle than childhood symptoms. Some specialists have suggested the following as a list of symptoms associated with ADHD in adults:

- Carelessness and lack of attention to detail
- Continually starting new tasks before finishing old ones
- Poor organizational skills
- Inability to focus or prioritize
- Continually losing or misplacing things
- Forgetfulness
- Restlessness and edginess
- Difficulty keeping quiet, and speaking out of turn
- Blurting out responses and often interrupting others
- Mood swings, irritability, and a quick temper
- Inability to deal with stress
- Extreme impatience
- Taking risks in activities, often with little or no regard for personal safety or the safety of others – for example, driving dangerously.

Related Conditions In Adults With ADHD

As with ADHD in children and teenagers, ADHD in adults can occur alongside several related problems or conditions. One of the most common is depression. Other conditions that adults may have alongside ADHD include:

1. **Personality Disorders:** Conditions in which an individual differs significantly from the average person in terms of how they think, perceive, feel or relate to others

2. **Bipolar Disorder:** A condition affecting your mood, which can swing from one extreme to another

3. **Obsessive-Compulsive Disorder (OCD):** A condition that causes obsessive thoughts and compulsive behavior

The behavioral problems associated with ADHD can also cause problems such as difficulties with relationships and social interaction.

Living With

Caring for a child with attention deficit hyperactivity disorder (ADHD) can be draining. The impulsive, fearless, and chaotic behaviors typical of ADHD can make everyday activities exhausting and stressful.

1. **Ways To Cope**

Although it can be difficult at times, it's important to remember that children with ADHD cannot help their behavior. People with ADHD find it difficult to suppress impulses, which means they do not stop considering a situation or the consequences before they act. If you're looking after a child with ADHD, you may find the below advice helpful.

2. Plan The Day

Plan the day, so your child knows what to expect. Set routines can make a difference in how a child with ADHD copes with everyday life. For example, if your child has to get ready for school, break it down into structured steps so they know exactly what they need to do.

3. Set Clear Boundaries

Make sure everyone knows what behavior is expected, and reinforce positive behavior with immediate praise or rewards. Be clear, using enforceable consequences, such as taking away a privilege, if boundaries are overstepped, and follow these through consistently.

4. Be Positive

Give specific praise. Instead of saying a general: "Thanks for doing that," you could say: "You washed the dishes well. Thank you."

These will make it clear to your child that you're pleased and why.

5. Giving Instructions

If you're asking your child to do something, give brief instructions and be specific. Instead of asking: "Can you tidy your bedroom?" say: "Please put your toys into the box and put the books back onto the shelf." This clarifies what your child needs to do and creates opportunities for praise when they get it right.

6. Incentive Scheme

Set up your incentive scheme using a points or star chart, so good behavior can earn a privilege. For example, behaving well on a shopping trip will earn your child time on the computer or some sort of game. Involve your child in it and allow them to help decide what the privileges will be. These charts need regular changes, or they become boring. Targets should be:

- Immediate – for example, daily
- Intermediate – for example, weekly
- Long-term – for example, 3-monthly

Try to focus on just 1 or 2 behaviors at a time.

7. Intervene Early

Watch for warning signs. If your child looks like they're becoming frustrated, overstimulated, and about to lose self-control, intervene. Distract your child, if possible, by taking them away from the situation. These may calm them down.

8. Social Situations

Keep social situations short and sweet. Invite friends to play, but keep playtimes short so your child does not lose self-control. Do not aim to do this when your child feels tired or hungry, such as after a school day.

9. Exercise

Make sure your child gets lots of physical activity during the day. Walking, skipping, and playing sport can help your child wear themselves out and improve their sleep quality. Make sure they're not doing anything too strenuous or exciting near to bedtime.

10. Eating

Keep an eye on what your child eats. If your child is hyperactive after eating certain foods, which may contain additives or caffeine, keep a diary of these and discuss them with a GP.

11. Bedtime

Stick to a routine. Ensure your child goes to bed at the same time each night and gets up at the same time in the morning. Avoid overstimulating activities in the hours before bedtime, such as computer games or watching TV.

12. Night Time

Sleep problems and ADHD can be a vicious circle. ADHD can lead to sleep problems, which in turn can make symptoms worse. Many children with ADHD will repeatedly get up after being put to bed and have interrupted sleep patterns. Trying a sleep-friendly routine can help your child and make bedtime less of a battleground.

Signs And Symptoms Of ADHD In Girls

Attention deficit hyperactivity disorder (ADHD) has long been thought of as a condition affecting males. But, more girls are being diagnosed as the understanding of the condition deepens. Girls are more likely to have inattentive ADHD, in which daydreaming and shyness are common, whereas it is more typical for boys to have hyperactive-impulsive ADHD or combined Presentation.

Living with undiagnosed ADHD can result in disadvantages, such as a lack of accommodations in the classroom, low self-esteem, and self-blame. Gone undiagnosed, ADHD can even affect mental health well into adolescence and adulthood. Being aware of the different ways ADHD can present in your daughter can help you know when it might be time to see a doctor for an evaluation.

Diagnosing ADHD In Girls

ADHD symptoms can manifest very differently in each child. You may have a boy who has been diagnosed with ADHD but never considered that your daughter, who is having trouble in school, might also have it too because her issues seem so different from his. It is much easier to identify a physically active and defiant child as someone who would benefit from an ADHD evaluation than someone who seems distant or distracted. In girls, ADHD signs and symptoms tend to have these underlying commonalities:

1. Compensates For Inattention

For many girls with ADHD, paying attention to the task at hand is their biggest challenge. They can get distracted by external events or drift off into a world of their own. For example, a bird outside a classroom window may take attention away from something more important in their environment, like a teacher announcing an upcoming exam date.

2. Always In Motion

If a hyperactive girl, she might be described as a "tomboy" because she likes physical activity and doesn't seem to enjoy the "typical things" a girl her age does. She might also be in motion in less obvious ways, perhaps doodling constantly or moving around in her chair.

3. Lack Of Impulse Control

A girl with impulsivity can be hyper-talkative and verbally impulsive, interrupting others, talking excessively, or changing topics again and again during conversations. She might blurt out words without thinking about their impact on others. But this girl may also be overly sensitive. Some girls are described as overemotional and easily excitable.

Signs And Symptoms

Not all girls with ADHD will exhibit all of the following signs and symptoms. Conversely, having one or two of these does not equal an ADHD diagnosis in and of itself. However, if your daughter seems to exhibit a few of these symptoms continually, a discussion with an experienced professional may be beneficial.

- Appears withdrawn
- Cries easily
- Daydreaming and in a world of her own
- Difficulty maintaining focus; easily distracted
- Disorganized and messy (in her appearance and physical space)
- Doesn't appear to be trying
- Doesn't seem motivated
- Forgetful
- Highly sensitive to noise, fabrics, and emotions
- Hyper-talkative (always has lots to say, but is not good at listening)
- Hyperreactivity (exaggerated emotional responses)
- Looks to be making "careless" mistakes
- Might often slam her doors shut
- Often late (poor time management)
- Problems completing tasks
- Seems shy
- Seems to get easily upset

- Shifting focus from one activity to another
- Takes time to process information and directions; seems like she doesn't hear you
- Verbally impulsive; blurts out and interrupts others

Seeking Help

If ADHD is diagnosed, it can be treated and managed. Interventions can be put in place, including behavior management techniques, organizational strategies, medication, counseling, and support. Simply knowing she has ADHD can relieve a girl of a huge burden of guilt and shame. It can also free her from the damaging labels of being "spacey," "unmotivated," "stupid," or "lazy." She is none of those things; she simply has ADHD. Strategies can be put in place to make life a little easier and her future much brighter.

Myths About ADHD

Myth 1: ADHD Is Not A Real Disorder

One factor contributing to misunderstandings about ADHD's status is that no specific test exists to identify the disorder definitively. Unlike other medical conditions, a doctor cannot confirm a diagnosis of ADHD with a laboratory or imaging test.

Although there is no definitive medical test for diagnosing ADHD, there are clear and specific criteria that must be met for a diagnosis. Doctors and mental health professionals can use these criteria and in-depth history, and detailed information about a person's behaviors to make a reliable diagnosis.

Another factor is that ADHD symptoms are not always clearly defined. ADHD exists on a continuum of behaviors. We all experience problems with attention and focus at times, but for an individual with ADHD, these symptoms are severe enough to affect daily functioning.

Symptoms of ADHD can also resemble those of other conditions. Pre-existing or undiagnosed medical conditions that could cause a person's symptoms must be ruled out before diagnosing ADHD can be made.

Myth 2: ADHD Is Over-Diagnosed

The evidence is mixed on whether ADHD is over-diagnosed. Annual data from the National Survey of Children's Health has shown an increase in ADHD diagnosis in U.S. children. However, the reports also demonstrate that rates of other conditions, such as autism, anxiety, and depression, have increased.

Specific to ADHD, several studies have shown that the condition may be under-diagnosed in cases where symptoms are less noticeable. A particular example comes from evidence that ADHD may manifest differently in female children.

While girls with ADHD might be less likely to display hyperactive physical symptoms, they can still have significant impairment with mental tasks and focus. Several studies have suggested that girls are less likely to be diagnosed and receive ADHD than their male peers.

Other studies have proposed that ADHD is over-diagnosed in children, but specifically in male children. Higher rates of ADHD in boys could partly be due to stereotypes about male behavior (boys act out physically). Boys may also be more likely to demonstrate overt and disruptive symptoms of ADHD, which in turn increases the likelihood that parents, teachers, and doctors will notice these behaviors.

Research has shown that racial, ethnic, and socioeconomic factors also influence the disparity in diagnosis and treatment of ADHD. Children in minority groups and those who live in poverty often lack equitable access to health care, including mental health services.

Research has also proposed that adult ADHD is over-diagnosed. It's been suggested that an adult might be diagnosed with ADHD due to the "medicalization" of typical life experiences and personality variations. In some cases, other mental health conditions or learning disabilities are misdiagnosed as ADHD.

Conversely, for adults who go undiagnosed and untreated, social stigma, stereotypes about ADHD, and cultural factors can make someone reluctant to seek (or accept) the diagnosis.

The main risk associated with the over-diagnosis of ADHD in children and adults is unnecessary treatment with stimulant medications. While these drugs can be an effective treatment for ADHD, they may be misused when prescribed to someone who does not need them.

Myth 3: ADHD Is Caused By Poor Parenting

Parents of children with ADHD may worry that they are somehow to blame for their child's behavior, but the condition is not strictly caused by poor parenting. While any child, whether they have ADHD or not, can be adversely affected by a chaotic home or parenting that is punitive and critical. These factors can make it more difficult for children and their families to cope with ADHD, but they don't cause the condition. That said, parents may want to consider adapting their parenting style to better support a child with ADHD.

Myth 4: Only Children Can Have ADHD

The symptoms of ADHD must be present by the age of seven to meet the criteria for diagnosis, but many individuals remain undiagnosed until adulthood. It's not uncommon for a parent to be diagnosed around the same time that their child is. As adults learn more about the condition, they may begin to recognize

ADHD traits and behaviors in themselves. Thinking back on their childhood, they may realize that the struggles they had at school were likely the result of attention problems that were not noticed or treated.

For parents and children, a diagnosis at any age often comes as a relief. Being able to put a name to the symptoms and knowing that there is a way to manage them can be reassuring.

Many children diagnosed with ADHD will continue to have symptoms as teens and adults, but the symptoms may change as they get older. For example, hyperactive behaviors common in kids tend to decrease with age, whereas restlessness, distractibility, and inattention may persist into adulthood.

Adults with ADHD that is poorly managed often experience chronic difficulties at work and in relationships. Undiagnosed and untreated ADHD is also associated with anxiety, depression, and substance misuse.

Myth 5: Hyperactivity Is Always A Symptom

The "attention deficit" part of the name has led to misunderstandings about the nature of ADHD and perpetuated myths about its symptoms. There are different types of ADHD, including:

- Predominately hyperactive-impulsive
- Predominately inattentive

- Combined

Hyperactive behaviors occur in the predominantly hyperactive-impulsive type but are not included in the predominately inattentive type. To reduce confusion, the predominantly inattentive type of ADHD is referred to as attention-deficit disorder (ADD).

A person with inattentive symptoms may appear daydreamy and easily distracted. They may be disorganized, forgetful, or careless. This type of ADHD is more likely to be overlooked, as it is less disruptive to others than the hyperactive type. However, the symptoms are still distressing to the person experiencing them.

While a child with ADHD won't typically outgrow the disorder, adults sometimes report "growing out of" the hyperactive behaviors they had as children.

Myth 6: People With ADHD Can't Focus At All

Given the condition's name, it can be confusing for people to see someone with ADD/ADHD focusing intently on an activity. It's more accurate to describe the "attention-deficit" portion of ADHD as difficulty regulating attention rather than the ability to pay attention. Although people with ADHD typically have trouble focusing on, organizing, and completing tasks, it's not uncommon for them to become absorbed in activities that interest them. Such a sustained level of hyperfocus can be a clue that someone has ADHD.

Myth 7: Medication Can Cure ADHD

Medication does not cure ADHD, but it can help manage symptoms when prescribed by a doctor or mental health professional. ADHD is a chronic, lifelong condition. If someone was prescribed ADHD medication as a child, they might need to continue taking it as an adult (though the dose may need to be adjusted).

People may have the same symptoms as adults that they did as children, or their symptoms may change or lessen over time. Developmental changes in the brain partly explain these changes, but they can also reflect how someone has learned to cope.

People with ADHD often develop coping strategies and organizational skills that help them live with the condition. They can continue building and expanding these skills throughout their lives and may choose to pair them with medication.

Myth 8: Stimulants Lead To Drug Abuse And Addiction

There is a concern that stimulant medications used to treat ADHD can lead to substance misuse. However, research has shown that untreated ADHD increases a person's risk for substance use disorder. Anxiety or depression are more likely to develop from untreated ADHD. A person may misuse licit and illicit drugs to self-medicate both their ADHD symptoms and those of secondary mental health conditions.

Associated Conditions Of Adhd

Other Concerns And Conditions With Adhd

ADHD often occurs with other disorders. Many children with ADHD have other disorders and ADHD, such as behavior or conduct problems, learning disorders, anxiety, and depression. The combination of ADHD with other disorders often presents extra challenges for children, parents, educators, and healthcare providers.

Therefore, healthcare providers need to screen every child with ADHD for other disorders and problems. This page provides an overview of the more common conditions and concerns that can occur with ADHD. Talk with your healthcare provider if you have concerns about your child's symptoms.

1. Behavior Or Conduct Problems

Children occasionally act angry or defiant around adults or respond aggressively when they are upset. When these behaviors persist over time or are severe, they can become a behavior disorder. Children with ADHD are more likely than other children to be diagnosed with a behavior disorder such as Oppositional Defiant Disorder or Conduct Disorder.

2. Oppositional Defiant Disorder

When children act out persistently so that it causes serious problems at home, in school, or with peers, they may be diagnosed with Oppositional Defiant Disorder (ODD). ODD is one of the most common disorders occurring with ADHD. ODD usually starts before eight years of age but can also occur in adolescents. Children with ODD may be most likely to act oppositional or defiant around people they know well, such as family members or a regular care provider. Children with ODD show these behaviors more often than other children their age. Examples of ODD behaviors include

- Often losing their temper
- Arguing with adults or refusing to comply with adults' rules or requests
- Often getting angry, being resentful, or wanting to hurt someone who they feel has hurt them or caused problems for them
- Deliberately annoying others; easily becoming annoyed with others
- Often blaming other people for their own mistakes or misbehavior

3. Conduct Disorder

Conduct Disorder (CD) is diagnosed when children show a behavioral pattern of aggression toward others, and serious violations of rules and social norms at home, school, and peers. These behaviors can lead to breaking the law and being jailed. Having ADHD makes a child more likely to be diagnosed with CD.

Children with CD are more likely than other children to get injured and to have difficulties getting along with peers. Examples of CD behaviors include:

- Breaking serious rules, such as running away, staying out at night when told not to, or skipping school
- Being aggressive in a way that causes harm, such as bullying, fighting, or being cruel to animals
- Lying and stealing, or damaging other people's property on purpose.

Treatment For Disruptive Behavior Disorders

Starting treatment early is important. Treatment is most effective if it fits the needs of the child and family. The first step to treatment is to have a comprehensive evaluation by a mental health professional. Some of the signs of behavior problems, such as not following rules, are also signs of ADHD, so it is important to get a careful evaluation to see if a child has both conditions. For younger children, the treatment with the strongest evidence is behavioral parent training. A therapist helps the parent learn effective ways to strengthen the parent-child relationship and respond to the child's behavior. For school-age children and teens, an often-used effective treatment is combination training and therapy that includes the child, the family, and the school. Sometimes medication is part of the treatment.

4. Learning Disorder

Attention-deficit hyperactivity disorder (ADHD) is not a learning disability; however, it does make learning difficult. For example, it is hard to learn when you struggle to focus on what your teacher says or when you can't seem to sit down and pay attention to a book.

ADHD and Learning Disabilities

Learning involves using the executive functions brain, particularly focusing, paying attention, engaging with a task, and using working memory. We know that ADHD affects the executive functions of the brain."

Many children with ADHD also have a learning disorder (LD). This is in addition to other symptoms of ADHD, such as difficulties paying attention, staying on task, or being organized, which can also keep a child from doing well in school. Having a learning disorder means that a child has a clear difficulty in one or more areas of learning, even when their intelligence is not affected.

When a person has coexisting conditions of ADHD and LD, it means they have the broad impairment of executive functions combined with the impairment of the particular skills needed for reading, writing, and math

What Are Learning Disabilities?

Learning disabilities are neurological and not a reflection of your child's intelligence or how hard you are trying. A popular way to describe LDs is that your brain is wired differently, and you receive and process information in a different way.

Learning disabilities can make reading, writing, spelling, and math difficult. They can also affect your ability to organize and recall information, listen and speak, and impact your short-term and long-term memory and timing.

The term learning disabilities is a collective term for a range of specific learning challenges. Learning disabilities are not problems with learning due to vision or hearing problems or learning in a second language.

People with learning disabilities often have average or above-average intelligence, yet there is a discrepancy between their achievements and potential. However, with the right support and interventions, they can close that gap and demonstrate their skills.

Examples Of Learning Disabilities

- Dyslexia: Reading disorder
- Dyscalculia: Math disorder
- Dysgraphia: Writing disorder
- Dyspraxia: Problems with motor skills

- Dysphasia/Aphasia: Problems with language
- Auditory processing disorder
- Visual processing disorder

The combination of problems caused by having ADHD and LD can make it particularly hard for a child to succeed in school. Properly diagnosing each disorder is an important part of getting the right kind of help for the child.

Impact

Learning disabilities are often discovered in school because of problems with academic work. However, their effects go beyond the classroom walls. They can impact family relationships and life at home and work.

Besides, learning disabilities affect a child's self-esteem. There is a general assumption that if someone is smart, they do well in school. However, this is not necessarily the case for someone who has an LD and ADHD. A learning disability means a pupil experiences problems with learning and demonstrating their knowledge traditionally.

Besides, pupils with ADHD have difficulty conforming to schools' exemplary behavior, such as sitting still for long periods and paying attention without acting impulsively or daydreaming. A pupil realizes they cannot do the tasks that other children seem to be done easily. They can feel isolated and different.

Diagnosis

When a person has more than one condition, it can be harder to recognize a second condition because they can mask each other. If you already have an ADHD diagnosis, it can be easy to attribute all your challenges to ADHD. In the same way that ADHD presents itself differently in everyone, so do learning disabilities, which makes recognizing them harder, there is not a definitive checklist. Like ADHD, there is a strong genetic component to learning disabilities. If you or your partner have an LD, your children could have one too.

Remember, knowledge is power. Learn as much as possible about learning disabilities and ADHD. If you or your child have already been diagnosed with ADHD and are following a treatment plan but still facing challenges, it could be that there is another condition present.

Who Can Make A Diagnosis?

Different specialists are qualified to test and diagnose different conditions. There might be variations depending on where you live and an individual clinician's qualification.

- **Child psychiatrist**: They can evaluate for ADHD but not an LD.
- **Clinical psychologist**: They can evaluate for both ADHD and LD.

- **Educational psychologist**: They can evaluate for an LD and, depending on their training, can evaluate for ADHD.
- **Neuropsychologists**: They can evaluate for both ADHD and LD.
- **School psychologists**: If they are working in a school, they can evaluate for an LD but not ADHD. However, if they are seen privately outside of school, they might evaluate for and diagnose ADHD.

Treating Both ADHD and LD

It is important to treat both ADHD and LDs. For example, if your child is on medication to help with their ADHD, their learning disability problems will persist. Or if they are receiving assistance for their LD, they will not get the full benefit if they struggle with their focus and impulsivity.

Treatment For Learning Disorders

Children with learning disorders often need extra help and instruction that is specialized for them. Having a learning disorder can qualify a child for special education services in school. Because children with ADHD often have difficulty in school, the first step is a careful evaluation to see if a learning disorder also causes the problems. Schools usually do their testing to see if a child needs intervention. Parents, healthcare providers, and the school can work together to find the right referrals and treatment.

5. Anxiety And Depression

Anxiety

Many children have fears and worries. However, when children experience so many fears and worries that they interfere with school, home, or play activities, it is an anxiety disorder. Children with ADHD are more likely than those without to develop an anxiety disorder. Examples of anxiety disorders include:

- **Separation Anxiety:** Being very afraid when they are away from family
- **Social Anxiety:** Being very afraid of school and other places where they may meet people
- **General Anxiety:** Being very worried about the future and about bad things happening to them

Depression

Occasionally being sad or feeling hopeless is a part of every child's life. When children feel persistent sadness and hopelessness, it can cause problems. Children with ADHD are more likely than children without ADHD to develop childhood depression. Children may be more likely to feel hopeless and sad when they can't control their ADHD symptoms, and the symptoms interfere with doing well at school or getting along with family and friends. Examples of behaviors often seen when children are depressed include:

- Feeling sad or hopeless a lot of the time
- Not wanting to do fun things
- Having a hard time focusing
- Feeling worthless or useless

Children with ADHD often have a hard time focusing on things that are not very interesting to them. Depression can make it hard to focus on normally fun things. Changes in eating and sleeping habits can also be a sign of depression. For children with ADHD who take medication, eating and sleeping changes can also be side-effects from the medication rather than signs of depression. Talk with your healthcare provider if you have concerns. Extreme depression can lead to thoughts of suicide.

Treatment For Anxiety And Depression

The first step to treatment is to talk with a healthcare provider to get an evaluation. Some signs of depression, like having a hard time focusing, are also signs of ADHD, so it is important to get a careful evaluation to see if a child has both conditions.

A mental health professional can develop a therapy plan that works best for the child and family. Early treatment is important and can include child therapy, family therapy, or a combination of both. The school can also be included in therapy programs. For very young children, involving parents in treatment is very important. Cognitive-behavioral therapy is one form of therapy used to treat anxiety or depression, particularly in older children.

It helps the child change negative thoughts into more positive, effective ways of thinking. Consultation with a health provider can help determine if medication should also be part of the treatment.

6. Difficult Peer Relationships

ADHD can make peer relationships or friendships very difficult. Having friends is important to children's well-being and may be very important to their long-term development. Although some children with ADHD have no trouble getting along with other children, others have difficulty in their relationships with their peers; for example, they might not have close friends or might even be rejected by other children. Children who have difficulty making friends might also more likely have anxiety, behavioral and mood disorders, substance abuse, or delinquency as teenagers.

How Does ADHD Interfere With Peer Relationships?

Exactly how ADHD contributes to social problems is not fully understood. Inattentive children sometimes seem shy or withdrawn from their peers. Their peers may reject children with symptoms of impulsivity/hyperactivity because they are intrusive, may not wait their turn, or may act aggressively. Also, children with ADHD are more likely than those without ADHD to have other disorders that interfere with getting along with others.

Having ADHD Does Not Mean A Child Won't Have Friends.

Not everyone with ADHD has difficulty getting along with others. For those children who do have difficulty, many things can be done to help them with relationships. The earlier a child's difficulties with peers are noticed, the more successful intervention may be. Although researchers don't have definitive answers on what works best for children with ADHD, some things parents might consider as they help their child build and strengthen peer relationships are:

- Pay attention to how children get along with peers. These relationships can be just as important as grades to school success.

- Regularly talk with people who play important roles in your child's life (such as teachers, school counselors, after-school activity leaders, healthcare providers, etc.). Keep updated on your child's social development in the community and school settings.

- Involve your child in activities with other children. Talk with other parents, sports coaches, and other involved adults about any progress or problems that may develop with your child.

- Peer programs can be helpful, particularly for older children and teenagers. Social skills training alone has not shown to be effective, but peer programs where children practice getting along with others can help external icon. Schools and communities often have such programs available. You may want to talk to your healthcare provider and someone at your child's school about programs that might help.

7. Risk Of Injuries

Children and adolescents with ADHD are likely to get hurt more often and more severely than peers without ADHD. Research indicates that children with ADHD are significantly more likely to

- Get injured while walking or riding a bicycle
- Have head injuries
- Injure more than one part of their body
- Be hospitalized for unintentional poisoning
- Be admitted to intensive care units or have an injury resulting in disability

More research is needed to understand why children with ADHD get injured, but being inattentive and impulsive likely puts children at risk. For example, a young child with ADHD may not look for oncoming traffic while riding a bicycle or crossing the street or may do something dangerous without thinking of the possible consequences. Teenagers with ADHD who drive may take unnecessary risks may forget rules, or may not pay attention to traffic.

There are many ways to protect children from harm and keep them safe. Parents and other adults can take these steps to protect children with ADHD.

- Always have your child wear a helmet when riding a bike, skateboard, scooter, or skates. Remind children as often as necessary to watch for cars and teach them how to be safe around traffic.
- Supervise children when they are involved in activities or in places where injuries are more likely, such as climbing or in or around a swimming pool.
- Keep potentially harmful household products, medications, and tools out of the reach of young children.
- Teens with ADHD are at extra risk when driving. They need to be extra careful to avoid distractions like driving with other teens in the car, talking on a cell phone, texting, eating, or playing with the radio. Like all teens, they need to avoid alcohol and drug use and driving when tired.
- Parents should discuss the rules of the road, why they are important to follow, and the consequences of breaking them with their teens. Parents can create parent-teen driving agreements that put these rules in writing to set clear expectations and limits.

8. Autism Spectrum Disorders (ASD)

Autism Spectrum Disorders include a large range of disorders characterized by difficulties with social skills, communication, repetitive behaviors, routine changes, and how they experience different senses. There are many symptoms commonly seen in ADHD that are also seen in ASD. It has been estimated that approximately 1/3 of children diagnosed with ADHD also meet the criteria for ASD. Besides, having a diagnosis of ADHD has been shown to delay the diagnosis of ASD by up to 3 years. Due to this fact, it is important to think about ASD in any child with ADHD.

9. Tic Disorders

It is estimated that about 1/10 children with ADHD also have a tic disorder. Tics are involuntary, repetitive movements (eye blinking, head jerking, or lip-smacking) or sounds (sniffing, throat clearing, coughing) that are typically not rhythmic. There are several tic disorders, but the most recognized and severe disorder is Tourette Syndrome (TS). Tourette Syndrome includes a combination of both motor and vocal tics ongoing over time.

10. Mood Disorders

Mood disorders, including depression, bipolar disorder, and seasonal affective disorder, are common in people of all ages with ADHD. It has been estimated that around ¼ of children with ADHD and close to ½ of adults with ADHD have co-occurring mood disorders. It is essential to watch for signs of these disorders and seek treatment as needed.

The Link Between ADHD And Boredom

Feeling bored usually happens when nothing in your environment captures your interest or attention. Boredom might start with your mind, but it can quickly affect your body and emotions too.

For example, you might feel restless or tired, and your mood can plummet. Boredom is one thing people with ADHD fear the most and will go to great lengths to avoid.

Common Signs of Boredom

How many of these sound familiar?

- You hang up the phone if you are put on hold, even if you resolve an important issue in the middle.
- You eat something, even though you aren't hungry.
- You phone a person you don't like that much, to have someone to talk to.
- You delay going to bed until you are completely exhausted to avoid the boredom of lying in bed waiting to fall asleep.
- You create an argument with a service provider or someone you love.
- You act in a potentially dangerous way. For example, you overtake a slow driver even if it's not completely safe because driving behind them is boring.

The opposite of bored is interested, energized, and cheerful.

Adults with ADHD are always looking for new or stimulating things because gear and the brain work well when they are interested in something.

How to Avoid Boredom

Get to know yourself and your favorite ways to avoid boredom. Boredom busters include trying the new and different, spending time with people, doing adrenaline activities, taking risks, problem-solving, adding movement, being 'hands-on,' etc.

When you know your favorite ways, design your life around those things, so each day is interesting for you. This includes your job and how you approach the tasks in your job description, hobbies, and how you do the mundane tasks of life, such as housework.

Be Prepared

Life is full of delays, so have a variety of activities on hand. For example, if you are flying, take a visual magazine, a book that you can get engrossed in, as well as a puzzle book. Don't leave things to chance and hope there will be a good movie to watch or that you will be sitting next to someone entertaining.

Use a Timer

Using a timer can make even the dullest things interesting, as it creates a sense of urgency and excitement. Play games with yourself. For example, see if you can do all the washing up in 15 minutes.

Balance

It is good to have self-awareness that you don't like feeling bored and do what is in your power to avoid it. However, don't become too fearful of being bored that you will do anything to avoid it. This is how accidents happen. It is empowering to know you can sit with it for a few moments if you are bored. Meditation and exercise are two daily habits that help you to endure unexpected boring parts of your day.

How To Tolerate Boredom

Unfortunately, boredom is not something that can always be avoided. It is important to learn how to cope during these times to avoid behaviors that may not be adaptive or appropriate for the situation.

Find A Focus

During moments when you find yourself faced with boredom, look for something that you can focus on. Is there a problem you are facing that needs to be solved? Make a mental list of possible solutions. Finding a mental focus during these dull moments can help keep your mind off your boredom and use your time constructively.

Practice Mindfulness

It can also be helpful to engage in brief moments of conscious thought. Pay attention to how you are feeling at the moment. Spend a few moments just focusing on your thoughts as they happen. Try focusing on your breathing. If you find your mind wandering, bring your attention back to the present moment.

Daydream

If you find yourself really and truly bored with a dull, daily task (folding laundry, doing the dishes, etc.), try just letting your mind wander. This gives you the ability to think about things that bring your joy or spark your interest while still completing those monotonous jobs that simply need to get done.

Notes

ADHD can be dealing with boredom particularly difficult, but finding ways to cope with dull moments can help. Being prepared can be one of the best tools for coping with boredom.

When you have ADHD, keeping your attention on a task often means that it needs to be something you are interested in, that you want, or find challenging. When boredom hits, turning to an activity you enjoy or presenting a challenge can help give your brain the stimulation you need.

Chapter 2: Accepting Your Child's ADHD and Parenting a Child With ADHD

The ADHD Series: Accepting That Your Child Has ADHD

There are many obstacles to accepting your child's ADHD diagnosis. Grandparents, extended family, or even your spouse may insist that a lack of strict discipline causes your child's problems. They may blame you for your child's problems because they may have limited knowledge of ADHD. Or it may be difficult for you to accept that your child is not perfect and has a problem requiring intervention; it's even more difficult to accept when the problem can't be 'cured' and will never go away. The stigma surrounding ADHD is also a reason why many parents are reluctant to accept the diagnosis.

One of the biggest problems of being in denial is that it prevents timely intervention. Valuable time is lost when parents deny a situation that warrants attention. Research has amply demonstrated that when ADHD is left unaddressed, it is likely to develop other mental health issues, such as depression, anxiety, conduct disorder, and substance use problems.

Being in denial could also prevent you from examining your feelings about what having an ADHD child means to you. These unprocessed feelings can inevitably leak out in interactions with your child, often in unhelpful ways.

1. Acknowledge That You Have A Child With ADHD.

This starts with reflecting on the diagnosis and your reaction to it. You won't be able to genuinely support your child if you haven't explored your feelings. Ask yourself if your child's struggles are familiar or foreign to you. If familiar, how did you deal with these struggles yourself? If not, how do you feel about having a child who is different from you and has challenges with concentration, hyperactivity, or self-regulation? Most parents feel a roller-coaster of grief, anger, helplessness, frustration, worry, uncertainty, or embarrassment.

What Can You Do?

- Figure out what you feel. If you're feeling sad, give yourself time to mourn. It's okay to acknowledge that the path you had in mind for your child's future is now redrawn. Process your emotions to release their hold on you.
- Understand that it's not your fault. What you ate in pregnancy or how you disciplined him has nothing to do with his symptoms.

- ADHD is a genetic condition, and blaming yourself for his behavior only does a big disservice to yourself and your child.
- Seek out information from reliable sources. There are books, podcasts, articles, and websites, that will help you appreciate that ADHD is very common, 'normal,' and manageable.
- If your child's diagnosis makes you realize that your issues with concentration, memory, or emotional outbursts may have been ADHD, too, seek professional help from a qualified mental health professional, such as a clinical psychologist.

2. Find Out Your Child's Response To Getting An ADHD Diagnosis.

Again, for most children, it is a mixed bag. It could be a relief for some children to get a name for what they knew was different about them. For others, it indicates something is wrong with them. The visits to a 'doctor,' unfortunately, may not convey that ADHD is 'normal' after all, we go to a doctor when we are sick, and something isn't right. For most children, ADHD is a negative label.

What Can You Do?

- Find out how your child understands his behavior. Does he feel he is different from his peers? Is he able to see what may be difficult for him is easy for children his age (or vice versa)? What does he feel works well for him?

- Explore your child's understanding of his challenges since his view of his challenges may differ from yours. For example, he may not care that he cannot follow your 5-step instruction to clear up his table, but what may bother him is his difficulty remembering and recalling a poem for recitation in front of his class.

- Explain what ADHD is in age-appropriate terms. Once your child has received a professional diagnosis, even if the CP has explained to her about what ADHD is, she may still rely on you to explain the term to her in ways that make sense to her. When your child grasps the biology and the facts about ADHD, it can be a source of hope, empowerment, and collaboration.

- 'Bullet speed,' 'racecar brain,' 'fast-paced,' 'this minute only brain' are some terms that children had devised to refer to themselves when explained how ADHD wires their brains differently. It is a good idea to explore with your child his experience of having ADHD and develop a term that fits in with this experience, making him feel labeled or judged. So, instead of using a medical term that can feel scary or diseased to some children, you can help reduce the stress of the ADHD label by focusing on what's personal about it for your child.

3. Understand Your Child's Struggles.

It's not uncommon for parents and teachers of children with ADHD (whether diagnosed or not) to think that they are lazy and unmotivated. However, it is important to remember that the tasks or chores your child has to do may be hard or stressful for her. Children with ADHD have executive functioning deficits, which means that they may have trouble paying attention, organizing and planning, starting tasks and staying focused on them, and keeping track of what they're doing.

What Can You Do?

- Acknowledge that it's not a problem of willpower. Completing a seemingly simple task such as hanging the milk basket outside is a multi-step process that requires many executive functioning skills including remembering to do it all. It is also challenging for a child with ADHD to switch from one activity to another, especially if the latter requires the skills he lacks (or has been told he lacks). It's a good idea to break down tasks into smaller chunks and only assign one part of a task at a time. Also, give enough time for your child to switch from one activity to another.
- Acknowledge that it may be a fear of failure. No child wants to feel stupid or bad about themselves. But if the

task in front of your child creates stress for her or evokes fear of failure, she will want to avoid it. So, remember not to criticize how your child ends up completing the task. Praise the effort, even if the outcome doesn't meet your expectations. You could also brainstorm with your child and tailor chores to suit her needs.

- Don't compare your child to other neurotypical peers. "Your child wants to feel understood and accepted for who they are, even if they don't understand or accept themselves," "Meet your child where they are, not where we expect them to be. Letting your child have a say in the task you're assigning to them will go a long way in helping them own it."

- Empathize with your child. Let your child know that you understand what she must be going through.

4. Focus On Your Child's Strengths.

When your child receives a diagnosis of ADHD, it's easy to see her neuro differences as deficits. But it's extremely important to see your child through a strengths-based lens and focus on enhancing those strengths. That will help develop her confidence and self-esteem and add valuable skills to her basket.

What Can You Do?

- Notice when you highlight deficits. When you focus on your child's difficult behaviors ("He's very lazy. He just doesn't want to do anything."), that's all you (and others) see. It also prevents you and your child from recognizing and nurturing his strengths.

- Recognize when you're rigid. It is unhelpful to view your child's behavior through a lens of 'shoulds' ("She should be more organized" or "She should clean up after herself"). It's important to recognize your child's executive functioning difficulties and manage your expectations accordingly, even for chores or tasks that seem 'too easy for her age.

- Reflect on your child's strengths. Use a notebook to write down what you like about your child, what he does well (include special talents, interests, and hobbies), what you do for fun together, and how you show him that you are upset but still love him. Consider how you can help him enhance his strengths, how you can help him take his hobbies to the next level, and how you can keep fostering the connection with him even in the face of difficult moments.

Parenting Tips For ADHD

Raising a child with ADHD isn't like traditional childrearing. Normal rule-making and household routines can become almost impossible, depending on the type and severity of your child's symptoms, so you'll need to adopt different approaches. It can become frustrating to cope with some of the behaviors which result from your child's ADHD, but there are ways to make life easier.

Parents must accept the fact that children with ADHD have functionally different brains from those of other children. While children with ADHD can still learn what is acceptable and what isn't, their disorder does make them more prone to impulsive behavior.

Fostering a child's development with ADHD means that you will have to modify your behavior and learn to manage your child's behavior. Medication may be the first step in your child's treatment. Behavioral techniques for managing a child's ADHD symptoms must always be in place. By following these guidelines, you can limit destructive behavior and help your child overcome self-doubt.

Principles Of Behavior Management Therapy

There are two basic principles of behavior management therapy. The first is encouraging and rewarding good behavior (positive reinforcement). The second is removing rewards by following bad behavior with appropriate consequences, leading to the extinguishing of bad behavior (punishment, in behaviorist terms). You teach your child to understand that actions have consequences by establishing rules and clear outcomes for following or disobeying these rules. These principles must be followed in every area of a child's life. That means at home, in the classroom, and the social arena. Decide ahead of time which behaviors are acceptable and which are not

Behavioral modification aims to help your child consider the consequences of an action and control the impulse to act on it. This requires empathy, patience, affection, energy, and strength on the part of the parent. Parents must first decide which behaviors they will and won't tolerate. It's crucial to stick to these guidelines. Punishing a behavior one day and allowing it the next is harmful to a child's improvement. Some behaviors should always be unacceptable, like physical outbursts, refusal to get up in the morning, or unwillingness to turn off the television when told to do so.

Your child may have a hard time internalizing and enacting your guidelines. Rules should be simple and clear, and children should be rewarded for following them. This can be accomplished using a points system. For example, allow your child to accrue points for good behavior that can be redeemed for spending money, time in front of the TV, or a new video game. If you have a list of house rules, write them down and put them where they're easy to see.

Repetition and positive reinforcement can help your child better understand your rules.

Define The Rules, But Allow Some Flexibility

It's important to reward good behaviors and discourage destructive ones consistently, but you shouldn't be too strict with your child. Remember that children with ADHD may not adapt to change as well as others. You must learn to allow your child to make mistakes as they learn. Odd behaviors that aren't detrimental to your child or anyone else should be accepted as part of your child's personality. It's ultimately harmful to discourage a child's quirky behaviors just because you think they are unusual.

Manage Aggression

Aggressive outbursts from children with ADHD can be a common problem. "Time-out" is an effective way to calm both you and your overactive child. If your child acts out in public, they should be immediately removed calmly and decisively. "Time-out" should be explained to the child as a period to cool off and think about the negative behavior they have exhibited. Try to ignore mildly disruptive behaviors as a way for your child to release his or her pent-up energy. However, destructive, abusive, or intentionally disruptive behavior which goes against the rules you establish should always be punished.

Parenting A Child With ADHD

While ADHD is believed to be hereditary, effectively managing your child's symptoms can affect both the disorder's severity and the development of more serious problems over time. Early intervention holds the key to positive outcomes for your child. The earlier you address your child's problems, the more likely you will be able to prevent school and social failure and associated problems such as underachievement and poor self-esteem that may lead to delinquency or drug and alcohol abuse. Although life with your child may seem challenging, as a parent, you can help create home and school environments that improve your child's chances for success.

Here Are Some Ways To Get Started.

1. **Don't Waste Your Limited Emotional Energy On Self-Blame:** ADHD is a disorder in certain areas of the brain and is inherited in the majority of cases. It is not caused by poor parenting or a chaotic home environment, although the home environment can make the symptoms of ADHD better or worse.

2. **Learn All You Can About ADHD:** While a great deal of information on the diagnosis and treatment of ADHD is available, not all are accurate or based on scientific evidence. It is up to you to be a good consumer and learn to distinguish accurate information from inaccurate. How can you sort out what will be useful and what will not? In general, it is good to be wary about ads claiming to cure ADHD. There is no cure for ADHD, but you can take positive steps to decrease its impact.

3. **Make Sure Your Child Has A Comprehensive Assessment:** To complete the diagnostic process, make sure your child has a comprehensive assessment that includes medical, educational, and psychological evaluations (involving input from your child's teacher) and that other disorders that either mimic or commonly occur with ADHD have been considered and ruled out.

How To Help Your Child Succeed At School

1. **Become An Effective Case Manager:** Keep a record of all information about your child. This includes copies of all report cards, teacher notes, disciplinary reports, evaluations, and documents from any meetings concerning your child. You might also include information about ADHD, a record of your child's prior treatments and

placements, and contact information for the professionals who have worked with your child.

2. **Form A Team That Understands ADHD And Be The Team Captain:** Meetings at your child's school should be attended by the principal's designee and a special educator, and a classroom teacher who knows your child. You, however, have the right to request input at these meetings from others that understand ADHD or your child's special needs. These include your child's physician, the school psychologist, and the nurse or guidance counselor from your child's school. If you have consulted other professionals, such as a psychiatrist, psychologist, educational advocate, or behavior management specialist, the useful information they have provided should also be made available at these meetings. A thorough understanding of your child's strengths and weaknesses and how ADHD affects him or her will help you and members of the team go on to develop an appropriate and effective program that takes into account his or her ADHD.

3. **Learn All You Can About ADHD And Your Child's Educational Rights:** The more knowledge you have about your child's rights under the two education laws, the Individuals with Disabilities Education Act (IDEA) and

Section 504 of the Rehabilitation Act, the better to maximize his or her success.

4. **Become Your Child's Best Advocate:** You need to represent and protect your child's best interest in school situations, both academic and behavioral. Become an active part of the team that determines what services and placements your child receives in an Individualized Education Plan (IEP) or Section 504 plan. See Education for Individuals with ADHD for more information.

5. **Communicate Regularly:** Adopt a collaborative attitude when working with your child's team. After all, everyone has the same goal, to see your child succeed! Let your child's teachers know if some major changes are going on in your family since your child's behavior can be affected. Invite the teachers to contact you with any issues or concerns before they become a problem. Having open lines of communication between you and the school will help your child.

How To Make Life At Home Easier

1. **Join A Support Group:** Parents will find additional information, as well as support, by attending local CHADD

meetings where available. You can find the nearest chapter to your home using the chapter locator.

2. **Seek Professional Help:** Ask for help from mental health professionals, particularly if you feel depressed, frustrated, or exhausted. Helping yourself feel less stressed will benefit your child as well.

3. **Work Together:** All of the adults that care for your child (parents, grandparents, relatives, and babysitters) must agree on how to handle your child's problem behaviors. Working with a professional, if needed, can help you better understand how to work together to support your child.

4. **Learn The Tools Of Successful Behavior Management:** Behavioral techniques have been widely established as a key component of treatment for children with ADHD. Parent training will teach you strategies to change behaviors and improve your relationship with your child. CHADD offers the Parent to Parent Program, which provides basic education on many facets of ADHD.

5. **Find Out If You Have ADHD:** Since ADHD is often inherited, many children with ADHD discover that they have ADHD when their child is diagnosed. Parents with ADHD may need the same evaluation and treatment types to seek their children to function at their best. ADHD in

the parent may make the home more chaotic and affect a parent's ability to be proactive rather than reactive.

Parent Training Will Help You Learn To:

1. **Provide Clear, Consistent Expectations, Directions, And Limits:** Children with ADHD need to know exactly what others expect from them. They do not perform well in ambiguous situations that don't specify exactly what is expected and that require them to "read between the lines." Working with a professional can help narrow the focus to a few specific behaviors, help you set limits, and consistently follow through with consequences.

2. **Set Up An Effective Discipline System:** Parents should learn proactive, not reactive, discipline methods that teach and reward appropriate behavior and respond to misbehavior with alternatives such as time-outs or loss of privileges. Communicate with the other people who care for your child and work to be as consistent with behavioral techniques across settings and caregivers as possible.

3. **Help Your Child Learn From His Or Her Mistakes:** At times, negative consequences will arise naturally out of a child's behavior. However, children with ADHD have

difficulty making the connection between their behaviors and these consequences. Parents can help their child with ADHD make these connections and learn from his/her mistakes.

How To Boost Your Child's Confidence

1. **Set Aside A Daily Special Time For You And Your Child:** Constant negative feedback can erode a child's self-esteem. Whether it's an outing, playing games, or just time spent with your child in positive interaction, a special time can help fortify your child against assaults to self-worth.

2. **Notice Your Child's Successes, No Matter How Small:** Make an effort to notice when your child is paying attention well or doing what s/he is supposed to be doing. Tell your child exactly what she/he did well. This can improve your child's self-esteem and teach him/her to notice gradual improvements, rather than being too hard on him/herself.

3. **Tell Your Child That You Love And Support Him/Her Unconditionally:** There will be days when you may not believe this yourself. Those will be the days when it is even more important that you acknowledge the difficulties your child constantly faces and express your

love. Let your child know that you will get through both the smooth and rough times together.

4. **Assist Your Child With Social Skills:** Peers may reject children with ADHD because of hyperactive, impulsive, or aggressive behaviors. Parent training can help you learn how to assist your child in making friends and learning to work cooperatively with others.

5. **Identify Your Child's Strengths:** Many children with ADHD have strengths in certain areas such as art, athletics, computers, or mechanical ability. Build upon these strengths so that your child will have a sense of pride and accomplishment. Make sure that your child has the opportunity to be successful while pursuing these activities and that untreated ADHD does not undermine his strengths.

Parenting A Child With ADHD

Children with ADHD are often bright, spontaneous, and caring. But parenting them is not without its challenges. Behavioral problems from forgetting to do chores to outright defiance can be frustrating for parents to navigate, as can low self-esteem, difficulty making friends, and the emotional ups and downs characteristic of ADHD.

To help their children navigate a world that isn't always friendly to those with developmental delays or mental health challenges, parents should advocate strongly for their children's needs, particularly in the classroom, encourage them to pursue their passions, and make sure their child feels loved, supported, and secure. Talking openly about ADHD, and seeking treatment if necessary, can also give the child the tools he needs to become his self-advocate as he grows up.

Why Is My Child With ADHD So Defiant?

Defiant behavior is often linked to ADHD, particularly in children whose symptoms are primarily hyperactive. Impulsivity may result in reckless or seemingly aggressive behaviors, while emotional dysregulation and an inability to rein in anger may be another root cause of defiance. In some cases, children with ADHD qualify to diagnose and oppositional defiant disorder, or ODD, a condition characterized by persistent negative, antagonistic behavior. Harsh discipline rarely works for these children; instead, practicing compassion and focusing on skill-building are the strategies most often recommended by experts.

What Is The Most Effective Discipline For A Child With ADHD?

Children with ADHD, like others, benefit from fair and consistent discipline. Experts recommend an approach that focuses on setting clear expectations, employing natural consequences, making sure consequences are enforced consistently, and praising positive behaviors. It's also best to avoid punishing children for behaviors out of their control and problematic behaviors with children to understand their motivation better. Behavior that seems to be defiant, for instance, may stem from frustration or anxiety; addressing the feelings that are behind the behavior will likely help mitigate outbursts in the future.

Will Rewards Help Change My Child's Behavior?

There are pros and cons to using formal reward systems such as sticker charts to motivate a child to behave. On the one hand, many parents have found that sticker charts or other reward systems help their child reduce problematic behaviors; this is especially likely when they are achievable, specific, and measured over the short term.

On the other hand, some parents worry that using rewards to encourage good behavior is akin to bribery. Some have found that it cultivates a negative "what's in it for me" attitude among children. Whether to use a sticker chart or other formal reward system is a personal decision; other, less structured rewards such as a surprise outing after a week of good behavior or a few words of genuine praise may be enough to motivate children without diminishing their intrinsic motivation to behave appropriately.

How Can I Help My Child Make Friends?

Unfortunately, some children with ADHD may struggle to make and keep friends often due to aggressive or hyperactive behavior, emotional outbursts, or the seeming inability to stay focused on a game or conversation. To help a child develop social skills, parents should gently but explicitly explain appropriate behavior. In these perhaps role-playing situations, the child often slips up, such as when she's losing at a game, offers praise when the child succeeds, and focuses on individual friendships rather than trying to force a child to fit into a larger group. Keeping playdates short, before frustration or hyperactivity set in, can also help children end social interactions on a positive note and build up their social reputation.

Is My Child Addicted To Video Games?

While experts continue to debate whether excessive video game use can truly be considered an "addiction," it's undeniable that many children with ADHD exhibit problematic behavior when it comes to video games. Video games are designed to be engaging and provide immediate rewards; children with ADHD may hyperfocus on them even to the point where they become seemingly oblivious to the world around them and may be more prone to become irritable or angry told to stop playing. Some children may also prefer video games to other activities, like sports or schoolwork, particularly if those are areas in which they struggle. If your child plays video games for hours each day, has little interest in other activities, or becomes enraged or inconsolable when limits are set, she has likely developed a problematic relationship with gaming that should be addressed.

My Child Only Has Younger Friends. Why?

It's common and OK for a child with ADHD to form friendships with younger children primarily. Since ADHD is a developmental delay, they may find that younger friends are closer to their maturity level. Additionally, younger friends may allow a child with ADHD to feel like the leader, which they may not experience in other domains, particularly if they struggle socially with same-age peers.

How Can I Set Limits On My Child's Video Game Play?

Rather than setting overly harsh rules on video game playing or taking away the games altogether, both of which can lead to conflict and resentment, parents may be better served by a more balanced approach. Allowing a certain amount of playing while also making sure that their child is engaging in other activities like exercise, creative play, or reading will minimize tension and allow children to reap some of the potential benefits of video gaming. If rules are set around gameplay, be consistent about enforcing them.

Why Does My Child Say He Feels Worthless?

Trouble making friends struggles at school or constantly being scolded for "bad" behavior can wreak havoc on a child's self-esteem with ADHD. It can be devastating for parents to hear their children say negative things about themselves or come to believe that they are incapable of success. While low self-esteem is a common and reversible side effect of ADHD, parents must, and persistent low self-esteem and feelings of worthlessness may be signs of a problem that extends beyond ADHD and may require additional intervention.

What Can I Do To Help Build My Child's Self-Esteem?

Parents can help cultivate self-esteem by offering real, genuine praise when a child succeeds; it's also beneficial to encourage her to pursue her interests to find domains in which she excels. A child who likes to doodle, for instance, may become a talented artist, while a child drawn to cooking may feel his confidence grow as he learns to master more complicated recipes. Gradually increasing her autonomy and making sure that she learns critical skills as she grows can also increase her sense of competence and self-assuredness. Ensuring your child has strong relationships, whether with family members, same-age peers, or trusted adults, can go a long way toward building lasting self-esteem.

What Sports Are Best For Children With ADHD?

Children with ADHD can excel at any sport (or other activity), particularly if they're highly interested in it and intrinsically motivated to participate. For children who are unsure what sport they'd like to try, however, or who have struggled with activities in the past, parents may find that individual sports like swimming, tennis, or martial arts are ideal for allowing children to get the benefits of exercise while mitigating the social challenges that come with team sports.

How Can I Help My Child With ADHD Go To Sleep?

Some research suggests that as many as 70 percent of children with ADHD have clinical sleep disturbances, including difficulty falling asleep, waking up frequently during the night, or waking up too early in the morning. Children may also resist going to bed in the first place, becoming defiant or upset at bedtime. Parents should establish a consistent bedtime routine to counteract sleep problems and create a soothing sleep environment with minimal distractions. They should make sure their child gets regular exercise and eats a healthy diet, both of which can greatly improve sleep. If sleep problems are severe, parents may wish to try melatonin supplements.

Keep in mind that stimulant medications may disrupt sleep, especially if a dose is taken later in the day; if you suspect this may be the culprit for your child's poor sleep, talk to your doctor about reducing the dose or changing the dosing schedule.

Does ADHD Ever Go Away?

ADHD is a life-long condition. That might seem like bad news if you are struggling right now. However! Take heart because there are people who are treating and managing their ADHD so well. They think it must have disappeared. The common theme is these people created a life that works to their advantage. For some people, this happened by a happy accident, while others worked hard to design their life to suit them.

Here are some tips so that you can do this too!

1. People

Spend time with people who think you are awesome just the way you are now. Avoid or minimize time with people who are critical of you or put you down. When you are trying to avoid criticism by being on your best behavior, your ADHD gets worse.

In contrast, when you are relaxed and happy, ADHD symptoms seem to improve. Rather than spending time with people who grumble about how much energy you have, spend time with people that are impressed by it or have even more energy than you do. If you love to talk, find people who enjoy that about you. Some people are shy and quiet and find making conversation hard work. Their favorite type of person is someone who loves to talk.

Some people get upset by ADHD behavior because it triggers an emotional wound in them. For example, if they are sensitive about being rejected, they will be deeply hurt if you don't phone them as much as they phone you, or if you forget a birthday or arrive late.

2. Lifestyle

Fill your life with things that help ADHD naturally. These include daily exercise, an ADHD-friendly breakfast, an Omega 3 supplement, and meditation. The trick to doing these things every day is either make them so fun you can't wait to do them or get them to be part of your routine where they happen automatically, like brushing your teeth.

3. Systems And Structure

Develop systems, habits, and structures that support you.

Having systems sounds grand, but they are simply things that help you feel organized. For example, if, like many ADHDers, you have trouble remembering things, you can develop systems to support your memory. One of the Untapped Brilliance blog readers described a system she created to help her remember important belongings before leaving her house.

"I have a little card with a list of essentials. I clip the card to my bag's handle when I'm home. That card reminds me, just before I leave, to check that everything is back in the bag where it belongs".

ADHDers resist structure because they think it reduces their creativity. However, the exact opposite is true. You can be much more creative within a structured framework.

Sometimes the people in your life can help provide a structured framework. For example, you and your spouse always go to bed at 11 p.m., or your friends have brunch together on a Sunday. Other times you create your structure, perhaps time to read or meditate.

4. Work Environment

Find a job you love and that suits you. Your work environment is an important area of your life because you spend a lot of your time there. If you can match your work environment with your unique strengths, personality, and how ADHD shows up for you, then your ADHD can seem to disappear.

If at school you were hyperactive and got into trouble for not being able to sit still or for talking to your friends, a job where you can move around a lot would be perfect, perhaps a sales job where you travel around and visit clients in their offices and no two days are the same. In contrast, working in an office and sitting at a desk for eight hours would be torture.

If you have inattentive ADHD, you might find it takes you slightly longer than others to perform a task. Rather than having a job where speed is required, work where your pace is seen as an asset. Instead of criticism, you would hear, "Wow, you are so conscientious and patient; you have all the time in the world for your clients."

Many people with ADHD struggle to wake up in the morning. Instead of working someplace where they start at 7:30 a.m. and being reprimanded for being late, work at jobs where there is flex time, or where the work culture starts later and finishes later than the traditional 8-4 or 9-5.

5. Your Mindset

When you are comfortable with yourself and your ADHD, it's easier to handle curve balls. You deal with them matter-of-factly. Suppose you lose your wallet, phone the bank and cancel your cards. If you forget where you parked your car, you look for it.

You don't get mad about it or talk so meanly to yourself that it takes weeks to recover. You manage your ADHD, learn strategies and tricks to help you. When something happens, you can trust yourself to handle it, and you don't see it as a personal failing.

Chapter 3: Pros And Cons Of ADHD and Tips For ADHD

Pros And Cons Of ADHD

People diagnosed with attention deficit hyperactivity disorder (ADHD) might sometimes be misunderstood. Most of the time, other individuals treat them differently because they think that having this type of disorder is hard to deal with. It was reported that children with ADHD are often being bullied and less likely to have many close friends or interact with peers. Parents also confirmed that there are deficits in a child's ability to get along with other children and adjust to new situations. Perhaps it would be better if people should take some time to understand their condition and begin to accept them as they are. Thus, here are a few pros and cons of ADHD that you might want to look into.

List of Pros Of ADHD

1. Multi-Talented Individual

These individuals can do things pretty well. They can do many sports and many hobbies that are too many to consider. Some of them can do notable things so well that others can't do them altogether, including calligraphy, drawing, Wing Chun martial arts, skateboarding, softball, and writing, among many other talents.

2. Being A Fast Reader

Some of these people can read books at a very fast pace in which they can finish from 5 to 10 books simultaneously in just a matter of one week. Likewise, they can finish reading regular novels of 250-350 pages in only a few hours.

3. Having Lots Of Thoughts And Ideas

Their ability to have lots of ideas or thoughts enables them to solve many problems for those who need it. This makes them excellent at assisting people in solving problems.

4. Being More Creative

The fact that they can create lots of solutions for certain problems also makes them creative at some point. For this reason, they can make some creative pieces and designs. Perhaps creativity is already in their genes.

5. Focused On One Thing Only

When it comes to doing and finishing a single task, it is their prerogative to pay attention to nothing but that particular task alone. As a result, they will have a high chance of completing a job at hand without worrying about other things.

List Of Cons Of ADHD

1. Bothersome Talents

The problem with having too many talents is that they cannot do one thing very well. Although they can do many things, they can just do it to a certain extent but not to a very talented level. So they can't master a single talent even though they are good at things.

2. Non-Stop Thoughts

Having too many thoughts and ideas can sometimes make them a bad conversationalist. This is because they can't filter a single thought at a time. This means that when they talk to someone, they have already been thinking of other things out of that current context.

3. A Bad Listener

Although they are good at helping other people, ADHD personalities can be poor listeners. Some of them have severe auditory focus impairment, making them unable to focus on lectures or people hosting the said events. For instance, he or she can't recall a conversation that happened a couple of minutes ago as it is his or her weakness not to pay attention to someone that he or she comes in contact with. However, there are instances when one can be better at textual communication as it is possible to recall everything through text messaging or email.

4. Offering Too Much Information

Having the disability of using a filter to any type of information can affect how they make a conversation. For instance, they cannot get to the point of their stories fast enough that they often drag the conversation in a long-winded manner. Some of them get to reveal too much about themselves in terms of relationships or friendships that are often taken advantage of by others.

5. Depression And Anxiety

Concerning ADHD, depression and anxiety can sometimes go hand in hand to disappoint. So whether they are alone or with lots of friends or acquaintances around, it is there to give them a very hard time. As a result, they get a lot of mood instability, self-doubt, and anxious thoughts to begin with.

6. Easily Gets Bored

Restlessness or easily gets bored is already part of those having ADHD. This means that some of them can't refrain from being restless. Most of the time, they can't help but become fidgety at something. At some point, they could have nervous energy in which they sadly can't productively release. Speaking of getting bored, their ability to get busy with tons of various hobbies explains it all. So when they lose interest in something, they move on easily to the next.

Pros And Cons Of ADHD Medication

ADHD is a problem that usually starts as a kid and can last until a person grows when not treated at once. Different medication options are offered for kids and adults with ADHD, and these treatments may include different effects, both good and bad. Whether a person with ADHD is still young or adult, experts who can use their professionalism with treatments for controlling any signs of ADHD are working hard on developing new treatments. Though many people are saying that these medications are what people with ADHD should get, there are still those who track such medications' pros and cons.

Pros Of ADHD Medication

The following are the main benefits of getting ADHD medications:

1. Behavioral Symptoms Are Reduced, Controlled, And Eliminated.

Given that people with ADHD are those with a short attention span and hyperactive, these medications help reduce, control, and eliminate whatever behavioral symptoms that people with the condition may show. As symptoms are controlled, people with the condition can improve their capabilities in other activities such as those regarding school.

2. Medications Are Not The Ones People Would Think Are Addicting.

All medications given to ADHD patients are not causing euphoria or make patients feel high because medications used are those that do not promote such effects.

3. ADHD People Are Given The Ability To Self-Regulate.

This is one of the abilities that people lack with the condition. Since it is already present in their peers, the medication will help them get the same self-regulation ability.

Cons Of ADHD Medication

As the positive side of the medication is given, it is time that people should also know the negative side of the medications that people with the condition are going through, and some of these are as follows:

1. May Cause Different Side Effects.

Since medications are given mostly to kids, making it difficult for them to withstand any side effects such as dizziness, sleepiness, and more, parents are worried about different side effects that people can get from the medication's continued use.

2. Continued Intake May Result In Psychological Dependency.

This is the part where the person would always rely on the medication whenever they would do something. It may lead to psychological dependency. A person will be afraid of doing anything because they forgot to take their medication or find it difficult to detach from the medication.

3. What You Should Think About ADHD Medication

With these pros and cons of the medication in mind, you can easily decide whether these will help a parent like you to handle your kids with ADHD or any of your love with the condition. You can now understand whether such medications are made to give a person with ADHD the opportunity to control his or her abilities or not.

Caring For A Child With ADHD: Tips

Bringing up a child with attention deficit hyperactivity disorder or ADHD comes with its challenges. There are no hard and fast rules, as ADHD can have different degrees of severity and symptoms. However, children can benefit from person-centered or tailor-made approaches.

ADHD can cause a child to have poor impulse control, leading to challenging or inappropriate behaviors. But an important step for parents is to accept that ADHD simply represents a functional difference in the brain. It does not mean that their child cannot learn right from wrong, but they may need to find other ways to support their child in developing positive behavior.

Parents and caregivers will need to adapt their ways of interacting with the child. This includes speech, gestures, emotional language, and the physical environment. For a child with ADHD, consistency is vital. Using a supportive and structured approach, challenging behaviors can be limited, and the child can flourish.

Tips For ADHD

The following tips have been compiled to help parents reduce disruptive behaviors and deal with challenges related to ADHD.

1. Keep It Interesting

When a child with ADHD is doing a complex task, they are less likely to become distracted. Children with ADHD often get distracted if a task is not challenging enough. This is called distractability. The opposite of distractability is hyperfocus, which is when a child is focused to unaware of their surroundings. Hyperfocus can also be challenging but can allow a child to get important tasks done.

2. Give Praise And Encouragement

Good behavior should be reinforced with praise. It is just as important for children with ADHD to learn what behaviors are acceptable by receiving praise as it is for them to learn what is unacceptable.

3. Provide Structure

Providing structure with a daily schedule may limit sudden distractions. Knowing what to expect can be calming for children with ADHD. It can also be a good way to introduce responsibility into a child's life.

4. Encourage Exercise

Burning off excess energy through exercise can help by:

- Lowering the risk of depression and anxiety
- Promoting concentration and focus
- Improving sleep patterns
- Stimulating the brain

Parents can encourage physical activity by providing active toys, such as balls and skipping ropes, teaching their children to ride a bike, or enrolling them in a team sport. Children are also more likely to develop physically active habits if their parents are good role models in this area. Going on family hikes or playing outdoors can help a child with ADHD expend excess energy and build healthy habits for the future.

5. Practice Good Sleep Hygiene

Research has shown that low-quality sleep can harm ADHD symptoms. Good quality sleep can help to regulate energy levels the next day. It can also improve stress and mood. To this end, parents may want to try and include regular bedtime hours into the day's structure.

6. Break Tasks Down

For someone with ADHD, some tasks can feel too complex and off-putting. Where possible, break tasks into achievable goals. As well as simplifying the picture, this can regulate the emotions associated with succeeding or failing.

7. Think Out Loud

Children with ADHD often lack impulse control. This means they may say or do something without thinking it through. Getting them to pause and say out loud what they are thinking can have several benefits. It can allow the parent to learn their child's thought patterns. It can also give the child time to consider their thought and whether or not to act on them.

8. Keep Distractions To A Minimum

If a child is easily distracted, it pays to keep their surroundings uncluttered. Depending on the child's preferences, radios or televisions could be turned down or off. Getting them to work on tasks away from the lure of TVs or games is important, and toys should be put away when they are doing something in their bedroom.

9. Explain Rather Than Command

A parent or caregiver can explain what they are asking, where it is age-appropriate for the child. Keep it simple but expect to be asked to elaborate. Explaining the reasons for doing a task can alleviate worry and confusion in a child with ADHD. When explaining things, a person should use positive and clear language. Explaining the reasons for asking the child to do a task is also respectful, and self-respect is crucial if they feel they may be different from others.

10. Introduce Wait Time

The idea behind wait time is similar to thinking out loud. If a child waits a few seconds before speaking or acting when they think, they have time to consider appropriate. This will take a lot of practice, but it can be worth it, and it can give them a real advantage in their social life.

11. Do Not Get Overwhelmed

When a parent is overly stressed, not only does their well-being suffer, but they can also be less effective in supporting their child. If a person's workload and obligations become overwhelming, it can be beneficial to ask for support. Friends, family, or local ADHD groups are potential sources of help. Even just dropping one thing from a person's weekly schedule can reduce stress.

12. Avoid Using Negative Language

Positive feedback can help build a child's confidence. A child with ADHD may feel that they are disliked or that they always do things wrong. Reinforcing this with negative language can be hurtful and make disruptive behaviors worse. It is impossible to be positive all the time, and so a parent needs to find an outlet to express their concerns or worries. This might be a friend, partner, or therapist. There are also online groups where parents of children with ADHD can discuss their challenges with people in similar situations.

13. Don't Allow ADHD To Be In Control

While some allowances can be made, ADHD does not excuse poor behavior. Children and parents both need boundaries, and children need to learn that there are always consequences when they misbehave. These consequences should be appropriate and consistent. If a child sees a parent does not always follow through on the consequences, this may encourage unruly behavior.

14. Pick Your Battles

Living with a child who may demonstrate hyperactive and impulsive behavior can be a constant challenge. If a parent addressed every problem, every day would be stressful and unpleasant for everyone. Learning to let the smaller things go can alleviate stress in the long term and help a parent focus on curbing the more important behaviors.

15. Do Not See Other Adults As The Enemy

It is natural for parents to feel protective, but when a child has ADHD, other caregivers do not understand them or do not care enough. Good communication can help solve this problem. It can help talk with anyone your child has contact with about ADHD, explain their preferences, and describe the most effective interventions for challenging behavior.

16. Keep Working On Modifying Behavior

If improvements to behavior stall or seem to have reached their limit, keep trying. Children with ADHD have huge potential. Perhaps a strategy needs to be tweaked or even just paused for a while. Children go through many developmental leaps, and sometimes they plateau. It is essential to be patient and keep trying to make positive changes, even if they take time.

17. Find Specialist Support

An ADHD therapist can help with parental stress in addition to a child's behaviors. As well as professional help, there are also many local and national support groups. Input from other parents in a similar situation can be invaluable.

18. Take Breaks

Spending the entire day focusing on any child can be exhausting. Take breaks where possible, either by arranging a babysitter or trading off responsibilities with a partner. The more energy a parent has, the better they can cope with stress.

19. Stay Calm

Remaining calm allows the brain to problem-solve and communicate better. There are many ways for a parent to stay calm in challenging situations. These strategies include:

- Meditating regularly
- Practicing yoga
- Sticking to a routine to eliminate the stress of "what next?"
- Walking in nature or other calming outdoor space
- Reducing caffeine and alcohol consumption

20. Remember That All Children Misbehave

It can be easy to think that ADHD causes all challenging behavior, but all children misbehave sometimes. Learn which behaviors need managing and which ones are normal parts of growing up.

Tips For ADHD: Do's And Don'ts

"Do's" For Coping With ADHD

1. Create Structure

Make a routine for your child and stick to it every day. Establish rituals around meals, homework, playtime, and bedtime. Simple daily tasks, such as having your child lay out his or her clothes for the next day, can provide essential structure.

2. Break Tasks Into Manageable Pieces

Try using a large wall calendar to help remind a child of their duties. Color coding chores and homework can keep your child from becoming overwhelmed with everyday tasks and school assignments.

3. Simplify And Organize Your Child's Life

Create a special, quiet space for your child to read, do homework, and take a break from the chaos of everyday life. Keep your home neat and organized so that your child knows where everything goes. This helps reduce unnecessary distractions.

4. Limit Distractions

Children with ADHD welcome easily accessible distractions. Television, video games, and the computer encourage impulsive behavior and should be regulated. By decreasing time with electronics and increasing time doing engaging activities outside the home, your child will have an outlet for built-up energy.

5. Encourage Exercise

Physical activity burns excess energy in healthy ways. It also helps a child focus their attention on specific movements. This may decrease impulsivity. Exercise may also improve concentration, decrease the risk for depression and anxiety, and stimulate the brain in healthy ways. Many professional athletes have ADHD. Experts believe that athletics can help children with ADHD find a constructive way to focus their passion, attention, and energy.

6. Regulate Sleep Patterns

Bedtime may be especially difficult for children who have ADHD. Lack of sleep exacerbates inattention, hyperactivity, and recklessness. Helping your child get better sleep is important. To help them get better rest, eliminate stimulants like sugar and caffeine, and decrease television time.

7. Encourage Out-Loud Thinking

Children with ADHD can lack self-control. This causes them to speak and act before thinking. Ask your child to verbalize their thoughts and reasoning when the urge to act out arises. It's important to understand your child's thought process to help him or her curb impulsive behaviors.

8. Believe In Your Child

Your child likely doesn't realize the stress that their condition can cause. It's important to remain positive and encouraging. Praise your child's good behavior, so they know when something was done right.

9. Take Breaks

You can't be supportive 100 percent of the time. It's normal to become overwhelmed or frustrated with yourself or your child. Just as your child will need to take breaks while studying, you'll need your breaks as well. Scheduling alone time is important for any parent. Consider hiring a babysitter. Good break options include:

- Going for a walk
- Going to the gym
- Taking a relaxing bath

10. Calm yourself

You can't help an impulsive child if you are aggravated. Children mimic the behaviors they see around them, so if you remain composed and controlled during an outburst, it will help your child to do the same. Take time to breathe, relax, and collect your thoughts before attempting to soothe your child. The calmer you are, the calmer your child will become.

"Don'ts" For Dealing With An ADHD Child

1. Don't Sweat The Small Stuff

Be willing to make some compromises with your child. If your child has accomplished two of the three chores you assigned, consider being flexible with the third, uncompleted task. It's a learning process, and even small steps count.

2. Don't Get Overwhelmed And Lash Out

Remember that a disorder causes your child's behavior. ADHD may not be visible on the outside, but it's a disability and should be treated as such. When you begin to feel angry or frustrated, remember that your child can't "snap out of it" or "just be normal."

3. Don't Be Negative

It sounds simplistic, but take things one day at a time and remember to keep it all in perspective. What is stressful or embarrassing today will fade away tomorrow.

4. Don't Let Your Child Or The Disorder Take Control

Remember that you are the parent and, ultimately, establish the rules for acceptable behavior in your home. Be patient and nurturing, but don't allow yourself to be bullied or intimidated by your child's behaviors.

Chapter 4: Improving The Social Skills Of Children With ADHD

How To Improve Social Skills In Children With ADHD

Having positive peer relationships and friendships is important for all children. Unfortunately, many kids with attention deficit hyperactivity disorder (ADHD) have difficulty making and keeping friends and being accepted within the larger peer group. The impulsiveness, hyperactivity, and inattention associated with ADHD can wreak havoc on a child's attempts to connect with others in positive ways.

Not being accepted by one's peer group, feeling isolated, different, unlikeable and alone, is perhaps the most painful aspect of ADHD-related impairments, and these experiences carry long-lasting effects. Positive connections with others are so important. Though kids with ADHD desperately want to make friends and be liked by the group, they often just don't know-how. The good news is that you can help your child develop these social skills and competencies.

Increasing Your Child's Social Awareness

Research finds that children with ADHD tend to be extremely poor monitors of their social behavior. They often do not have a clear understanding or awareness of social situations and the reactions they provoke in others. They may feel that an interaction with a peer went well, for example, when it did not. ADHD-related difficulties can result in weaknesses in this ability to accurately assess or "read" a social situation, self-evaluate, self-monitor, and adjust accordingly. These skills must be taught directly to your child.

Teach Skills Directly And Practice, Practice, Practice

Children with ADHD tend to have a hard time learning from past experiences. They often react without thinking through consequences. One way to help these kids is to provide immediate and frequent feedback about inappropriate behavior or social miscues. Role-playing can help teach, model, and practice positive social skills, as well as ways to respond to challenging situations like teasing.

Start by focusing on one or two areas your child is struggling with the most. This helps ensure the learning process doesn't become too overwhelming.

Many kids with ADHD have difficulty with the basics, like starting and maintaining a conversation or interacting with another person reciprocally (for example, listening, asking about the other child's ideas or feelings, taking turns in the conversation, or showing interest in the other child), negotiating and resolving conflicts as they arise, sharing, maintaining personal space, and even speaking in a normal tone of voice that isn't too loud.

Identify and give information to your child about social rules and the behaviors you want to see. Practice these prosocial skills again and again and again. Shape positive behaviors with immediate rewards.

Create Opportunities For Friendship Development

For preschool and elementary school-age children, play dates provide a wonderful opportunity for parents to coach and model positive peer interactions for their child and for the child to practice these new skills. Set up these playtimes between your child and one or two friends at a time, rather than a group of friends. Structure the playtime so that your child can be most successful.

Think of yourself as your child's "friendship coach." Carefully consider the length of time a playdate will run and choose activities to keep your child most interested.

As a child gets older, peer relationships and friendships are often more complicated. Still, it is equally important for you to continue to be involved and facilitate positive peer interactions. The middle school and high school years can be brutal for a child who struggles socially. Even if a child remains unaccepted by the peer group, having at least one good friend during these years can often protect the child from the full-on negative effects of ostracism by the peer group.

Research and get involved in your community groups that foster positive peer relationships and social skills development like Boy Scouts, Indian Guides, Girl Scouts, Girls on the Run, sports teams, etc. Ensure the group leaders or coaches are familiar with ADHD and can create a supportive and positive environment for learning prosocial skills.

Communicate with the school, coaches, and neighborhood parents to know what is going on with your child and with whom your child is spending time. A child's peer group and the characteristics of this group have a strong influence on the group's individuals.

Work With The School To Improve Peer Status

Once a child is labeled by his or her peer group negatively because of social skill deficits, it can be very hard to dispel this reputation. Having a negative reputation is perhaps one of the largest obstacles your child may have to overcome socially.

Studies have found that the negative peer status of children with ADHD is often already established by early-to-middle elementary school years. This reputation can stick with the child even as he or she begins to make positive changes in social skills.6 For this reason, it can be helpful for parents to work with their child's teachers, coaches, etc., to try to address these reputational effects.

Establish a positive working relationship with your child's teacher. Tell them about your child's areas of strength and interests, as well as what they've been struggling with. Share any strategies you've found helpful when working on your child's areas of weakness.

Young children often look to their teacher when forming social preferences about their peers. A teacher's warmth, patience, acceptance, and gentle redirection can serve as a model for the peer group and affect a child's social status.

When a child has experienced failures in the classroom, it becomes even more important for the child's teacher to consciously find ways to draw positive attention. One way to do this is to assign the child special tasks and responsibilities in the other children's presence in the classroom.

Make sure these are responsibilities in which your child can experience success and develop better self-worth and acceptance within the classroom. Doing this also provides opportunities for the peer group to view your child positively and may help stop the group process of peer rejection. Pairing the child up with a compassionate "buddy" within the classroom can also help facilitate social acceptance.

Collaborate with your child's teacher to make sure the classroom environment is as "ADHD-friendly" as possible so that your child is better able to manage ADHD symptoms. Work together with the teacher (and coach or another adult caregiver) on effective behavior management approaches and social skills training.

Medication, when appropriate, is often helpful in reducing the negative behaviors that peers find off-putting. If your child is on medication to help manage symptoms of ADHD, be sure to work closely and collaboratively with your child's doctor. For the medication to provide the optimal benefit that it can in helping to manage the core ADHD symptoms, there is often an ongoing need to monitor, fine-tune, and make adjustments along the way.

Helping A Child With ADHD Develop Social Skills

The emotional maturity level of children with attention deficit hyperactivity disorder (ADHD) may be well below that of their counterparts without ADHD. This means that a 10-year-old with ADHD may behave more like a 7- or 8-year-old around their peers, struggle to play well with others, and have a hard time sharing and losing games.

While children must be involved in activities with others, many children with ADHD have difficulty making and keeping friends. If a peer group doesn't accept a child, this can make them feel isolated, which can be one of the most painful parts of having ADHD. While some parents isolate their children from participating in activities with others, kids with ADHD must take part in social activities to help develop social skills.

Children with ADHD often have a harder time monitoring their social behavior than other children. They don't always know how to read social situations and others' reactions. Parents play an important role in helping increase self-awareness in children with ADHD.

Follow these tips to help your child improve his or her social skills:

Provide immediate, frequent feedback about inappropriate behavior and social miscues. Children with ADHD have difficulty monitoring their social behavior, so they may need someone to provide guidance. Role-playing with your child is an effective way to simulate situations that your child may encounter. You can also point out facial expressions, scenarios, and appropriate or inappropriate behavior in characters in books or TV.

Focus on a few areas that your child struggles with, such as listening or showing interest in another child. Explain to your child social rules and behaviors that reflect these skills. Set goals that are achievable and specific. Goals can be as simple as saying hi to a friend at the grocery store.

Schedule play dates with only one or two friends. This scenario usually is better for a child with ADHD than a play date with a large group of friends. Pair your child with children that are role models for good social skills.

Reward improved social skills, and reinforce skills that need more work.

One of the most effective ways to help your child develop social skills is to coach him or her at the moment and have your child participate in activities with their peers instead of isolating him or her from others. Practicing social skills with others is more effective than simply practicing in the office setting.

Chapter 4 : ADHD At School

ADHD And School

School can be a challenge for students with attention deficit hyperactivity disorder but here's how you can help your child or teen succeed in the classroom.

Setting Up Your Child For School Success

The classroom environment can pose challenges for a child with attention deficit hyperactivity disorder (ADHD or ADD). These students' very tasks find the most difficult sitting still, listening quietly, concentrating are the ones they are required to do all day long. Perhaps most frustrating of all is that most of these children want to learn and behave like their unaffected peers. Neurological deficits, not unwillingness, keep kids with attention deficit disorder from learning in traditional ways.

As a parent, you can help your child cope with these deficits and overcome the challenges school creates. You can work with your child to implement practical strategies for learning both inside and outside the classroom and communicate with teachers about how your child learns best. With consistent support, the following strategies can help your child enjoy learning, meet educational challengesn and experience success at school and beyond.

Tips For Working With Teachers

Remember that your child's teacher has a full plate: in addition to managing a group of children with distinct personalities and learning styles, they can also expect to have at least one student with ADHD.

Teachers may try their best to help your child with attention deficit disorder learn effectively, but parental involvement can dramatically improve your child's education. You have the power to optimize your child's chances for success by supporting the steps taken in the classroom. If you can work with and support your child's teacher, you can directly affect your child's experience with ADHD at school.

There are some ways you can work with teachers to keep your child on track at school. Together, you can help your child learn to find their feet in the classroom and work effectively through the school day's challenges. As a parent, you are your child's advocate. For your child to succeed in the classroom, you must communicate their needs to the adults at school. It is equally important for you to listen to what the teachers and other school officials have to say.

You can ensure that communication with your child's school is constructive and productive. Try to keep in mind that your mutual purpose is finding out how to help best your child succeed in school. Whether you talk over the phone, email, or meet in person, make an effort to be calm, specific, and above all, positive a good attitude can go a long way when communicating with the school.

1. Plan Ahead: You can arrange to speak with school officials or teachers before the school year even begins. If the year has started, plan to speak with a teacher or counselor on at least a monthly basis.

2. Make Meetings Happen: Agree on a time that works for both you and your child's teacher and stick to it. If it's convenient, meet in your child's classroom so you can get a sense of their physical learning environment.

3. Create Goals Together: Discuss your hopes for your child's school success. Together, write down specific and realistic goals and talk about how to help your child reach them.

4. Listen Carefully: Like you, your child's teacher wants to see them succeed at school. Listen to what they have to say even if it is sometimes hard to hear. Understanding your child's challenges in school is the key to finding solutions that work.

5. Share Information: You know your child's history, and your child's teacher sees them every day: together, you have a lot of information that can lead to a better understanding of your child's hardships. Share your observations freely, and encourage your child's teachers to do the same.

Developing And Using A Behavior Plan

Children with ADD/ADHD are capable of appropriate classroom behavior, but they need structure and clear expectations to keep their symptoms in check. As a parent, you can help develop a behavior plan for your child and sticking to it. Whatever type of behavior plan you decide to implement, create it in close collaboration with your child and their teacher.

Kids with attention deficit disorder respond best to specific goals and daily positive reinforcement as well as worthwhile rewards. Yes, you may have to hang a carrot on a stick to motivate your child to behave better in class. Create a plan that incorporates small rewards for small victories and larger rewards for bigger accomplishments.

Tips For Managing ADHD Symptoms At School

ADHD impacts each child's brain differently so that each case can look quite different in the classroom. Children with ADHD exhibit a range of symptoms: some seem to bounce off the walls, some daydream constantly, and others just can't seem to follow the rules.

As a parent, you can help your child reduce any or all of these types of behaviors. It is important to understand how attention deficit disorder affects different children's behavior to choose the appropriate strategies for tackling the problem. There are various fairly straightforward approaches you and your child's teacher can take to manage the symptoms of ADHD best—and put your child on the road to school success.

Managing Distractibility

Students with ADHD may become so easily distracted by noises, passersby, or their thoughts that they often miss vital classroom information. These children have trouble staying focused on tasks that require sustained mental effort. They may seem as if they're listening to you, but something gets in the way of their ability to retain the information. Helping kids who distract easily involves physical placement, increased movement, and breaking long stretches of work into shorter chunks.

- Seat the child with ADHD away from doors and windows. Put pets in another room or a corner while the student is working.
- Alternate seated activities with those that allow the child to move their body around the room. Whenever possible, incorporate physical movement into lessons.

- Write important information down where the child can easily read and reference it. Remind the student where the information is located.
- Divide big assignments into smaller ones, and allow children frequent breaks.

Reducing Interrupting

Kids with attention deficit disorder may struggle with controlling their impulses, so they often speak out of turn. In the classroom or at home, they call out or comment while others are speaking. Their outbursts may come across as aggressive or even rude, creating social problems as well. The self-esteem of children with ADHD is often quite fragile, so pointing this issue out in class or front of family members doesn't help the problem and may even make matters worse.

Correcting the interruptions of children with ADHD should be done carefully to maintain the child's self-esteem, especially in front of others. Develop a "secret language" with the child with ADHD. You can use discreet gestures or words you have previously agreed upon to let the child know they are interrupting. Praise the child for interruption-free conversations.

Managing Impulsivity

Children with ADHD may act before thinking, creating difficult social situations in addition to problems in the classroom. Kids who have trouble with impulse control may come off as aggressive or unruly. This is perhaps the most disruptive symptom of ADHD, particularly at school.

Methods for managing impulsivity include behavior plans, immediate discipline for infractions, and a plan for giving children with ADHD a sense of control over their day.

- Make sure a written behavior plan is near the student. You can even tape it to the wall or the child's desk.
- Give consequences immediately following misbehavior. Be specific in your explanation, making sure the child knows how they misbehaved.
- Recognize good behavior out loud. Be specific in your praise, making sure the child knows what they did right.
- Write the schedule for the day on the board or a piece of paper and cross off each item as it is completed. Children with impulse problems may gain a sense of control and feel calmer when they know what to expect.

Managing Fidgeting And Hyperactivity

Students with ADHD are often in constant physical motion. It may seem like a struggle for these children to stay in their seats. Kids with ADD/ADHD may jump, kick, twist, fidget, and otherwise move in ways that make them difficult to teach.

Strategies for combating hyperactivity consist of creative ways to allow the child with ADHD to move appropriately at appropriate times. Releasing energy this way may make it easier for the child to keep their body calmer during work time.

- Ask children with ADHD to run an errand or complete a task for you, even if it just means walking across the room to sharpen pencils or put dishes away.
- Encourage a child with ADHD to play a sport or at least run around before and after school and make sure the child never misses recess or P.E.
- Provide a stress ball, small toy, or another object for the child to squeeze or play with discreetly at their seat.
- Limit screen time in favor of time for movement.

Dealing With Trouble Following Directions

Difficulty following directions is a hallmark problem for many children with ADHD. These kids may look like they understand and might even write down directions but then aren't able to follow them as asked. Sometimes these students miss steps and turn in incomplete work or misunderstand an assignment altogether and wind up doing something else entirely.

Helping children with ADHD follow directions means taking measures to break down and reinforce the steps involved in your instructions and redirecting when necessary. Try keeping your instructions extremely brief, allowing the child to complete one step and then come back to find out what they should do next.

Tips For Making Learning Fun

One positive way to keep a child's attention focused on learning is to make the process fun. Using physical motion in a lesson, connecting dry facts to interesting trivia, or inventing silly songs that make details easier to remember can help your child enjoy learning and even reduce the symptoms of ADHD.

Helping Children With ADHD Enjoy Math

Children who have attention deficit disorder tend to think in a "concrete" manner. They often like to hold, touch, or take part in an experience to learn something new. By using games and objects to demonstrate mathematical concepts, you can show your child that math can be meaningful and fun.

1. Play Games: Use memory cards, dice, or dominoes to make numbers fun. Or simply use your fingers and toes, tucking them in or wiggling them when you add or subtract.

2. Draw Pictures. Especially for word problems, illustrations can help kids better understand mathematical concepts. If the word problem says there are twelve cars, help your child draw them from steering wheel to the trunk.

3. Invent Silly Acronyms: To remember the order of operations, for example, make up a song or phrase that uses the first letter of each operation in the correct order.

Helping Children With ADHD Enjoy Reading

There are many ways to make reading exciting, even if the skill itself tends to pose a struggle for children with ADHD. Keep in mind that reading at its most basic level involves stories and interesting information which all children enjoy.

1. Read To Children: Make reading cozy, quality time with you.

2. Make Predictions Or "Bets": Constantly ask the child what they think might happen next. Model prediction: "The girl in the story seems pretty brave, I bet she's going to try to save her family."

3. Act Out The Story: Let the child choose their character and assign you one, too. Use funny voices and costumes to bring it to life.

How Does Your Kid Like To Learn?

When children are given information that makes it easy for them to absorb, learning is a lot more fun. If you understand how your child with ADHD learns best, you can create enjoyable lessons that pack an informational punch.

1. Auditory Learners: Learn best by talking and listening. Have these kids recite facts to a favorite song. Let them pretend they are on a radio show and work with others often.

2. Visual Learners: Learn best through reading or observation. Let them have fun with different fonts on the computer and use colored flash cards to study. Allow them to write or draw their ideas on paper.

3. Tactile Learners: Learn best through physical touch or movement as part of a lesson. For these students, provide jellybeans for counters and costumes for acting out parts of literature or history. Let them use clay and make collages.

Tips For Mastering Homework

Sure, kids may universally dread it but for a parent of a child with ADHD, homework is a golden opportunity. Academic work done outside the classroom provides you as the parent with a chance to support your child directly. It's time you can help your child succeed at school where you both feel most comfortable: your living room. With your support, kids with ADHD can use homework time not only for math problems or writing essays but also for practicing the organizational and study skills they need to thrive in the classroom.

Helping A Child With ADHD Get Organized

When it comes to organization, it can help to get a fresh start. Even if it's not the start of the academic year, go shopping with your child and pick out school supplies that include folders, a three-ring binder, and color-coded dividers. Help the child file their papers into this new system.

- Establish a homework folder for finished homework and organize loose papers by color-coding folders. Show your child how to file appropriately.
- Help your child organize their belongings daily, including backpacks, folders, and even pockets.
- If possible, keep an extra set of textbooks and other materials at home.
- Help your child learn to make and use checklists, crossing items off as they accomplish them.

Helping A Child With ADHD Get Homework Done On Time

Understanding concepts and getting organized are two steps in the right direction, but homework also has to be completed in a single evening and turned in on time. Help a child with ADHD to the finish line with strategies that provide consistent structure.

- Pick a specific time and place for homework that is as free as possible of clutter, pets, and television.
- Allow the child breaks as often as every ten to twenty minutes.
- Teach a better understanding of the passage of time: use an analog clock and timers to monitor homework efficiency.

- Set up a homework procedure at school: establish a place where students can easily find their finished homework and pick a consistent time to hand in work to the teacher.

Other Ways To Help Your Child With Homework

1. Encourage exercise and sleep. Physical activity improves concentration and promotes brain growth. Importantly for children with ADHD, it also leads to better sleep, which can reduce the ADHD symptoms.

2. Help your child eat right. Scheduling regular nutritious meals and snacks while cutting back on junk and sugary foods can help manage symptoms of ADHD.

3. Take care of yourself, so you're better able to care for your child. Don't neglect your own needs. Try to eat right, exercise, get enough sleep, manage stress, and seek face-to-face support from family and friends.

Common Classroom Accommodations Which Are Extremely Helpful To Children With ADHD Include:

- Untimed tests
- Use of calculator or computer
- Modification of assignments
- Elimination of unnecessary writing write answers only, not questions
- Reduced demands on limited working memory capacity

- Written homework assignments were given by teachers
- The utilisation of note-takers or guided lecture notes

Accommodations should be individualized and made to accommodate each child's specific learning problems.

Other Factors Related To ADHD May Also Influence The Child's School Work:

1. Restlessness Or Hyperactivity In Younger Children: Can't sit still in the seat long enough to complete work.

2. Sleep Disturbances: Children may come to school feeling tired; may sleep in class. Many children with attention deficits (50%) have difficulty falling asleep at night and waking up each morning. Approximately half of them wake up tired even after a full night's sleep. Children may have battles with their parents before arriving at school. This suggests that there are problems with the neurotransmitter serotonin.

3. Medication Wears Off: With the advent of long-acting medications like Adderall XR, Concerta, and Strattera, problems with medication wearing off at school are less common. However, the effects of short-acting medications such as Ritalin or Dexedrine (regular tablets) wear off within three to four hours, and children may begin having trouble paying attention around ten or eleven o'clock in the morning. Even the intermediate-range medications (6-8 hours) like Ritalin SR, Dexedrine SR, Metadate ER, or Adderall may wear off by early afternoon. Class failure, irritability, or misbehavior may be linked to times when medication has worn off.

4. Low Frustration Tolerance: Children with attention deficits may become frustrated more easily, and "blow up" or impulsively say things they don't mean, especially as their medication is wearing off. They may blurt out answers in class. Or they may be argumentative or impulsively talk back to a teacher. Transitions or changes in routine, such as when substitute teachers are present, are also difficult.

Chapter 6 : Behavioral Therapy

What Is Behavioral Therapy?

Behavioral therapy is a term used to describe a broad range of techniques used to change maladaptive behaviors. The goal is to reinforce desirable behaviors and eliminate unwanted ones. Behavioral therapy is rooted in behaviorism principles, a school of thought focused on the idea that we learn from our environment.

Unlike some other therapy types that are rooted in insight (such as psychoanalytic therapy and humanistic therapies), behavioral therapy is action-based. Because of this, behavioral therapy tends to be highly focused. The behavior itself is the problem, and the goal is to teach people new behaviors to minimize or eliminate the issue.

Types Of Behavioral Therapy

There are some different types of behavioral therapy. The type of therapy used can depend on various factors, including the condition that is being treated and the severity of the symptoms. Applied behavior analysis uses operant conditioning to shape and modify problematic behaviors.

- **Cognitive-Behavioral Therapy (CBT):** Relies on behavioral techniques but adds a cognitive element, focusing on the disturbing thoughts behind behaviors.
- **Dialectical Behavioral Therapy:** Is a form of CBT that utilizes behavioral and cognitive techniques to help people learn to manage their emotions, cope with distress, and improve interpersonal relationships.
- **Exposure Therapy:** Utilizes behavioral techniques to help people overcome their fears of situations or objects. This approach incorporates techniques that expose people to the source of their fears while practicing relaxation strategies. It is useful for treating specific phobias and other forms of anxiety.
- **Rational Emotive Behavior Therapy (REBT):** Focuses on identifying negative or destructive thoughts and feelings. People then actively challenge those thoughts and replace them with more rational, realistic ones.
- **Social Learning:** Theory centers on how people learn through observation. Observing others being rewarded or punished for their actions can lead to learning and behavior change.

Techniques

To understand how behavioral therapy works, it is important to know more about the basic principles that contribute to behavioral therapy. The techniques used in this type of treatment are based on classical conditioning and operant conditioning theories.

Techniques Based On Classical Conditioning

Classical conditioning involves forming associations between stimuli. Previously neutral stimuli are paired with a stimulus that naturally and automatically evokes a response. After repeated pairings, an association is formed, and the previously neutral stimulus will come to evoke the response on its own.

Classical conditioning is one way to alter behavior. Several different techniques and strategies are used in this approach to therapy.

1. **Aversion Therapy:** This process involves pairing an undesirable behavior with an aversive stimulus hoping that the unwanted behavior will eventually be reduced. For example, someone with an alcohol use disorder might take disulfiram, a drug that causes severe symptoms (such as headaches, nausea, anxiety, and vomiting) when combined with alcohol.

2. **Flooding:** This process involves exposing people to fear-invoking objects or situations intensely and rapidly. It is often used to treat phobias. During the process, the individual is prevented from escaping or avoiding the situation.

3. **Systematic Desensitization:** In this technique, people list fears and then learn to relax while concentrating on these fears. Starting with the least fear-inducing item and working their way up to the most fear-inducing item, people systematically confront these fears under the guidance of a therapist while maintaining a relaxed state. Systematic desensitization is often used to treat phobias and other anxiety disorders.

Techniques Based On Operant Conditioning

Operant conditioning focuses on how reinforcement and punishment can either increase or decrease the frequency of a behavior. Behaviors followed by desirable consequences are more likely to occur again in the future, while those followed by negative consequences become less likely to occur.

Behavioral therapy techniques use reinforcement, punishment, shaping, modeling, and related techniques to alter behavior. These methods benefit from being highly focused, which means that they can produce fast and effective results.

1. **Contingency Management:** This approach uses a formal written contract between a client and a therapist (or parent or teacher) that outlines behavior-change goals, reinforcements, rewards, and penalties. Contingency contracts can be very effective in producing behavior

changes since the rules are spelled out clearly, preventing both parties from backing down on their promises.

2. **Extinction:** Another way to produce behavior change is to stop reinforcing behavior to eliminate the response. Time-outs are a perfect example of the extinction process. During a time-out, a person is removed from a situation that provides reinforcement. By taking away what the person found rewarding, unwanted behavior is eventually extinguished.

3. **Modeling:** This technique involves learning through observation and modeling the behavior of others. Rather than relying simply on reinforcement or punishment, modeling allows individuals to learn new skills or acceptable behaviors by watching others perform those desired skills.

4. **Token Economies:** This strategy relies on reinforcement to modify behavior. People are allowed to earn tokens that can be exchanged for special privileges or desired items. Parents and teachers often use token economies, allowing kids to earn tokens for engaging in preferred behaviors and lose tokens for undesirable behaviors. These tokens can then be traded for rewards such as candy, toys, or extra time playing with a favorite toy.

Uses

Behavioral therapy can be utilized to treat a wide range of psychological conditions. Some of the disorders that behavioral therapy can be used to treat include:

- Anxiety
- Attention deficit hyperactivity disorder (ADHD)
- Autism spectrum disorders
- Bipolar disorder
- Borderline personality disorder (BPD)
- Depression
- Eating disorders
- Panic disorder
- Phobias
- Obsessive-compulsive disorder (OCD)

Behavioral therapy is problem-focused and action-oriented. For this reason, it can also be useful for addressing specific psychological concerns such as anger management and stress management.

Impact

Behavioral therapy is widely used and is effective in treating many different conditions. Cognitive-behavioral therapy, in particular, is often considered the "gold standard" in the treatment of many disorders.Research has shown that CBT is most effective for the treatment of:

- Anger issues
- Anxiety
- Bulimia
- Depression
- Somatic symptom disorder
- Stress
- Substance abuse

This does not mean that CBT or other behavioral approaches are the only therapy types that can treat mental illness. It also doesn't mean behavior therapy is the right choice for every situation.

Tips/Tricks

If you are interested in behavioral therapy, there are some things that you can do to get the most out of your treatment.

1. Find A Behavioral Therapist: Some mental health professionals who can provide behavioral therapy include counselors, psychologists, psychiatrists, and social workers.

2. Ask For Recommendations: If you aren't sure where to begin your search, it can be helpful to ask your primary care physician for a referral.

3. Set Goals: Once you begin treatment, discuss your goals. Knowing what you hope to accomplish can help you and your therapist creates an effective treatment plan.

4. Be An Active Participant: For behavioral therapy to be effective, you need to be committed to participating in the process.

Parent Training In Behavior Management For ADHD

Behavior therapy is an effective treatment for attention-deficit/hyperactivity disorder (ADHD) that can improve children's behavior, self-control, and self-esteem. It is most effective in young children when parents deliver it. Experts recommend that healthcare providers refer parents of children younger than 12 years old for training in behavior therapy. For children younger than six years old, parent training in behavior management should be tried before prescribing ADHD medicine.

When parents become trained in behavior therapy, they learn skills and strategies to help their child with ADHD succeed at school, at home, and in relationships. Learning and practicing behavior therapy requires time and effort, but it has lasting benefits for the child and the family.

What Should Parents Look For?

If possible, families should look for a therapist who focuses on training parents. Some therapists will have training or certification in a parent training program that has been proven to work in young children with ADHD.

Therapists may also use strategies like those in proven programs.The following list of questions can be used to find a therapist who uses a proven approach.

Does This Therapist

- Teach parents skills and strategies that use positive reinforcement, structure, and consistent discipline to manage their child's behavior?
- Teach parents positive ways to interact and communicate with their child?
- Assign activities for parents to practice with their child?
- Meet regularly with the family to monitor progress and provide coaching and support?
- Re-evaluate treatment plans and remain flexible enough to adjust strategies as needed?

What Can Parents Expect?

Parents typically attend eight or more sessions with a therapist. Sessions may involve working with groups of parents or with one family alone. The therapist regularly meets the parents to review their progress, provide support, and adjust strategies as needed to ensure improvement. Parents typically practice with their children between sessions.

Parents have the greatest influence on their young child's behavior. The only therapy that focuses on training parents is recommended for young children with ADHD because they are not mature enough to change their behavior without their parents' help. Some therapists may use play therapy or talk therapy to treat young children with ADHD. Play therapy provides a way for children to communicate their experiences and feelings through play. Talk therapy uses verbal communication between the child and a therapist to treat mental and emotional disorders. Neither of these has been proven to improve symptoms in young children with ADHD.

Learning and practicing behavior therapy requires time and effort, but it has lasting benefits for the child. Ask your healthcare provider about the benefits of parent training in behavior therapy for young children with ADHD.

The fundamentals of behavior therapy for ADHD are easy to understand and implement, even without a psychologist's help. Have you ever given your child a time-out for talking back, for instance, or a heads-up before taking him some place that is likely to challenge his self-control? Then you already have a sense of how behavior therapy works in parenting children with ADHD.

"A lot of behavior modification is just common-sense parenting," says William Pelham, Jr., Ph.D., director of the Center for Children and Families at the State University of New York at Buffalo. "The problem is that none of us were trained how to be good parents, and none of us expected to have children who needed parents with great parenting skills and patience."

Behavior therapy's basic idea is to set specific rules governing your child's behavior (nothing vague or too broad) and enforce your rules consistently, with positive consequences for following them and negative consequences for infractions. To get started on your own, Dr. Pelham suggests these seven strategies, based on real ADHD behavior therapy techniques:

1. Make Sure Your Child Understands The Rules.

Telling a child to "do this" or to "avoid doing that" is not enough. To ensure that your child knows the rules cold, create lists and post them around the house. For example, you might draw up a list detailing the specific things your child must do to get ready for school. Make sure the rules are worded clearly. Go over the rules to make sure he understands and review them as necessary. Stick with the routines until your child has them down and then stick with them some more; backsliding is a common phenomenon.

2. Give Clear Commands.

First, say your child's name to make sure you have his attention. Then tell him exactly what you want him to do. If you're in the checkout line at the grocery store, for instance, you might say, "Steve, stand next to me and do not touch anything." It's not enough to tell your child to "be good" because he may not know what that entails. Finally, state the consequences for disobeying the command and always follow through.

3. Don't Expect Perfection.

Strike a balance between praising your child and offering criticism. A good rule of thumb is to praise your child for doing something well three to five times as often as you criticize bad behavior. You'll only set your child up for failure if you expect immediate and perfect results. Instead, focus on rewarding small steps and gradually work your way toward the desired outcome. If you notice that you are criticizing too much, lower your standards a bit. You'll only drive yourself and your child crazy if you nitpick.

4. Set Up A Point/Token System For Rewards And Consequences.

One effective system for encouraging your child to comply with your commands involves a jar and a marble supply. Each time your child does what you ask, put a marble in the jar. Each time he doesn't, take one out of the jar. He earns a small reward based on the number of marbles that remain in the jar and then starts over again.

6. Tweak Your Discipline Techniques As Your Child Gets Older.

Certain measures, including time-outs, may not work well with tweens and teens as they do with younger kids. If your high-schooler breaks a rule, you might give him a five-minute chore such as straightening up the family room rather than a five-minute time-out. With older children, it's useful to negotiate the terms and rewards for good behavior. For example, your child may request access to the family car or time spent with friends if he is helpful around the house and does well at school.

7. Ask Your Child's Teachers To Set Up A Similar Behavioral System At School.

One of the best tools for parent-teacher cooperation is the daily report card. Meet with the teacher to determine desired classroom behaviors "completing assignments within the designated time" or "contributing to the discussion." At the end of each school day, the teacher can fill out a quick evaluation of your child's adherence to these behavioral goals and send the document home with the child. Reward him for a good day at school with time to play outside or control over the car radio. If your child is in middle school or high school, ask his guidance counselor to discuss a weekly report card with all of your child's teachers. Use pages in her assignment notebook for these regular reports.

Behavioral therapy is an effective method to help improve ADHD your child's behavior, self-esteem, and self-control. Behavior management, also called behavior modification, can make parenting a child with attention deficit hyperactivity disorder (ADHD) a little easier. Behavioral Therapy for ADHD treatment involves rewarding and praising your child's good behavior and discouraging unwanted or impulsive behavior with appropriate consequences. Cognitive-Behavioral Therapy (CBT for ADHD), in this regard, serves as the perfect example. The following are the steps to follow to achieve the best behavior out of your child:

1. Explain The Rules

Make your child aware of your house rules and implement them at school too. Post them in places where your child can read them. For example, on the refrigerator or a specific board assigned for reminders for your child. Constantly remind them these rules are meant to be followed. Explain every rule and repeat them so they are etched in their brains.

2. Do not expect perfection

You need to remember, we all make mistakes. Therefore, don't expect perfection from your child even after several attempts to improve their conditions. You cannot expect perfection from your child even if you have to repeat certain rules every day. The important thing to remember is that one day your child will learn and notice the little improvements he/she makes daily.

3. Reward Your Child For Good Behavior (Activities For Children With ADHD)

Rewarding is an effective way for children to remember that they did something right and got a treat or a reward for it. Allowing them to play outside or do favorite activities or snacks can be examples of rewards you can give your kid.

Children with ADHD need more immediate feedback for their good behavior and their unwanted behavior than other children. Children with ADHD may learn from praise for their good behavior long after it occurs. However, due to the short attention span of ADHD children, they need to be told right after performing good or bad to work on their behavior and improve.

4. Give Clear Commands

Do not pile up commands on your ADHD child. This is because of the forgetful nature of children with ADHD, making it hard for them to memorize instructions like other children. Instead, redirect your child towards their tasks every time they divert their attention from the given task. This will help them to work independently and to memorize their assigned activities.

How Behavior Therapy Works

When some people hear the term therapy, they may think of clients sitting with a therapist to talk about emotions and work through problems. Behavior therapy is very different from this, however. It focuses on a person's actions, not on thoughts and emotions.

Therapists, typically clinical psychologists, work with clients to create a plan to help change behavior. The plan is designed to replace negative habits and actions with positive ones.

Behavior therapy for kids is as much about changing the parents' behavior as the child's. Parents can get into the habit of nagging and yelling, reinforcing their child's negative actions. A big piece of behavior therapy is coaching parents on how to replace their negative actions with positive ones, too.

What To Expect From Behavior Therapy

So what can you expect from behavior therapy for ADHD? It starts with you, your child, and the therapist having a meeting.

Together, you'll talk about the behaviors that are most challenging at school or home. Those might be things like talking out of turn, not finishing homework, or having angry outbursts.

The therapist will help you develop a plan for you and your child to follow that addresses the most troublesome behaviors. The plans are based on a system of rewards and consequences. (That's why your child needs to be there. You'll need your child's help to come up with rewards that are motivating!)

Next, you'll create a chart listing the specific actions your child needs to take. These should be clear, concrete, and measurable, so your child knows exactly the expectations.

The chart can use pictures or words or both. It should be posted at home where your child can easily see and use it. The plan is that when kids do what they're supposed to do, you'll check it off. Then they earn points toward a reward.

Once you start using the chart, you'll meet with the psychologist every week without your child. The purpose of those sessions is to talk about how things are going, troubleshoot problems, and adjust the plan as needed. In essence, the therapist will be training you to be the "therapist" at home. Once a month, your child will join you at those sessions.

How Behavior Therapy Can Help Kids With ADHD

Behavior therapy can be helpful for lots of kids and adults, too. But it can be especially helpful for kids with ADHD. Kids with ADHD can struggle with self-control and anger, which can lead to problem behaviors. It's also not uncommon for kids with ADHD to lie frequently about everyday tasks like chores.

Behavior therapy takes a very businesslike approach to help kids with ADHD change how they act and respond to situations. One goal is to eliminate arguing at home and give kids the motivation to change without parents being so involved.

The point of behavior therapy is to replace negative behaviors with positive ones. So the system of rewards and consequences is very specific. But whatever the reward is, it's always coupled with praise to reinforce good behavior. (It's important that your child's teachers be aware of this plan. Then they can reinforce the behavior at school, too.)

Let's say one of the behaviors you want to change is putting off starting homework. On the chart, you'll put the desired behavior: "Start my homework when I'm supposed to."

You'll also decide on a reward. It might be: "For every five times I start on time, I'll get an extra hour of screen time." So each time your child does homework with only one cue from you, you'll mark it off, and your child will earn points.

Equally important are verbal recognition and praise from you. For instance, you might say, "You did a great job remembering to raise your hand in class. I'm pleased with how hard you're trying."

If kids don't remember to raise their hand, they simply don't get the point. But they don't get in trouble or lose any points. The point is to reward positive behavior and ignore negative behavior.

However, if this approach isn't successful, you might need to switch to negative consequences like losing points. And if the negative behavior you're trying to change is aggression, you might have to use negative consequences in that situation, too.

Behavior Therapy And School

Sometimes therapy targets in-school behavior. In those cases, teachers have to be part of the process. You'll need to get your child's teacher to agree to help enforce the behavior plan. You'll also need to make sure the plan is simple enough that it won't eat up too much of the teacher's time and attention.

It's important to know that therapy isn't always enough to help with ADHD symptoms. If your child is still struggling, talk to your child's health care provider. Together you can discuss whether to consider ADHD medication in addition to or instead of behavior therapy. You may also want to read about different professionals who help kids with ADHD.

Chapter 7: ADHD Skills

ADHD And Social Skills Training

Social skills training for children is an important and practical step in the comprehensive approach used to help children successfully manage their ADHD symptoms. All children crave socialization and acceptance, and those diagnosed with ADHD are no different. However, due to their ADHD symptoms, kids find this to be a challenge. Our ADHD program at Best Practice Psychiatry will help identify and address the underlying psychosocial causes of children's symptoms and work with them to develop these skills in a fun and relaxed environment.

Learning practical skills with a trained professional will help develop socialization areas that are often lacking and difficult for children with ADHD. It will help them learn to overcome their challenges with strength and strategic tools. With dedicated time on these skills, children can learn to interpret verbal and nonverbal cues, develop increased self-control, and better understand and manage the world around them.

Social skills training focuses on helping the child behave in a more socially acceptable way with a specific step-by-step approach. It helps them:

- Identify their triggers
- Increase frustration tolerance
- Develop interpersonal cooperation skills
- Assertiveness training
- Listening and conversation skills.

Additionally, children can learn to accept the consequences of their actions. Learning these skills will help children understand the impact of their behaviors, know the clear and specific ways to manage them, and provide them with opportunities to be successful in the future.

A CBT therapist will help the child understand the relationship between their thoughts, emotions, and behaviors to increase awareness, understanding and develop increased control over their actions. Counseling will help break down behaviors, thoughts, and emotions into smaller steps and help them understand their unique differences. The kids will also learn to modify and adjusting their behaviors at the moment to make socializing and interacting with others a more pleasurable experience.

Any new skill may be challenging to learn at first. However, with consistency, structure, and practice, any child can learn improved coping methods with their ADHD symptoms.

Strategies/Techniques For ADHD

- Study Skills
- Plan for longer study time.
- Find a quiet space that is used for studying only.
- Develop a routine.
- Take frequent breaks.
- Keep up with work and do not wait until the last minute to study.
- Allow extra time for writing assignments to includes editing & rewriting.
- Use tutors when necessary.
- Highlight or color code important information in text and notes.
- Rewrite notes.
- Test self on information studied, including making up practice essay questions.
- Use active reading techniques read headings before reading the chapter, skim chapter to see what comes next, takes notes while reading, makeup questions using chapter headings, practice answering these questions while reading, review major points.
- Use a laptop computer to take class notes.
- Space studying throughout the day into one-hour sessions rather than spending 3-4 hours in the evening.
- Find your prime study time when you are most attentive and at your best.

- Figure at what type of environment is best, white noise versus absolute quiet.

- Figure out if you study better alone so you won't get off track talking to others or if you need others around to make studying more interesting and help you stay on track.

- Review notes as soon after class as possible, filling in any gaps, and helping to remember the information, then review notes before the next class.

- Use the SQ4R method, Survey Question Read, Rite (write) Recite Review-survey sections by looking over the main headings, makeup questions, read the entire sections, rite answers to the questions, recite the information out loud if possible, and review your work.

- Use movement (reading, underlining, writing in margins, highlighting, stimulation, and conversation(reciting information out loud), to stay alert while studying.

Organizational Skills

- Keep desk clear of mess.

- Use folders/binders to organize class notes and study notes.

- Leave margins when taking notes to add information from the text.

- Keep track of books and other supplies.

- Get books and articles from the library before you sit down to write.
- Clear/straighten desk at the end of every day.

Time Management Skills

- Start each day with a list of what needs to be done and prioritize your goals; for example, buying socks does not have the same importance as completing your assignment due in class that day.
- Do not procrastinate.
- Finish the "to do" list each day.
- Do not overbook or overschedule.
- Allow extra time for assignments, readings, and studying.
- Organize time with space for breaks, rest, exercise, social time, and meals.
- Use a daily planner to write down all important tasks/activities for the day.
- Stick to the plan and avoid temptations of distracting activities.
- Be realistic about how long things will take and block off study time, lab work, library research, and writing time in a daily planner.
- Build-in an extra room in case things take longer than planned.

- Break down large tasks into small components and put these in the planner. A large task may feel overwhelming; however when it is broken down into small parts, each component is quite manageable.
- Do not use a "To Do" box. For people with ADHD, these become Never Done piles.
- Use an appointment book with a semester at a glance, month at a glance, and a week at a glance features.

Course/Assignment Strategies

- Develop a relationship with each professor and discuss needs.
- See the professor immediately if anything was missed in class.
- Take a break between classes to get a snack, walk around, sit and relax for a moment.
- Try to schedule classed carefully to allow enough time to get from one part of the campus to another.
- Alternate between harder/easier or challenging/less challenging courses and spread class load over 2-3 days (M, W, F are heavy, but T, Thu are light) to allow for study and writing time.
- Plan big papers to allow time to meet with the professor to discuss the topic, do library research, editing, rewriting, and organization, and use several drafts.

Test Preparation Strategies

- Review information frequently. This is the only way information is stored in long-term memory.
- Understand information rather than just rote memorization.

Structure

- Frequent use of lists and notes to self.
- Color code (e.g., files, texts, schedules).
- Consistent use of routines and rituals.
- Reminders.
- Computer software program that assists in managing time.
- Use of calendar, computers, phones.

Procrastination

- Stick to your daily plan.
- Do things that were put off from the day before.
- Tackle tough assignments early.
- Pick an interesting paper assignment to avoid boredom.
- Evaluate choice of major and seek help from advisor or career center.
- Learn what motivates you.
- Work before play.
- Use little rewards throughout the day (e.g., soda break, snacks, telephone calls, visiting a friend).

- Time breaks to avoid letting a 10-15 minute break turned into 30-45 minutes.
- Avoid the TV when studying; use this as a reward for finishing or plan to study around a tv break.
- Give bigger rewards for getting a paper done (e.g., weekend away from campus, game away from home).

Managing ADHD

ADHD isn't just about difficulty at work or school, and it also contributes to reduced self-esteem, troubled relationships, and even the likelihood of automobile accidents. Thankfully, a little bit can go a long way in the treatment of ADHD. For some, becoming aware of weaknesses, and developing strategies to counter them, can result in big improvements.

The Managing ADHD worksheet describes five key skills that can often help those with ADHD. The skills include: creating structure, setting aside time for relationships, staying organized, creating the right environment, and living a healthy lifestyle. Each section describes the importance of the skill and tips to implement it successfully.

We want to point out that this worksheet has a lot of content, which will be overwhelming if you try to cover too much at once. Try picking just one or two sections to focus on for an entire hour, and make sure your client leaves with something specific to practice before their next session.

Three Surprising Skills ADHD Affects

You may already know the major signs of ADHD. But it doesn't just impact focus and self-control. Here are three surprising skills ADHD can affect.

1. Managing Emotions

Emotions can feel more intense with ADHD. They can even get in the way of everyday life. People with ADHD may be quick to get frustrated by seemingly minor things. And they might have trouble calming down when they're angry or upset. Learn more about ADHD and:

- Anxiety
- Mood swings
- Coping with grief
- Remorse

2. Getting Things Done

The ADHD brain makes it hard for people to get organized and get things done. It's especially hard to get started on tasks they have little or no interest in. This isn't a matter of willpower. It's about how ADHD affects brain chemistry.

3. Hyperfocus

ADHD can make it hard to focus. But it can also make it hard for people to stop focusing on something they really enjoy, like playing a video game. ADHD can also make it hard to stop thinking about something that's worrying them. That's because ADHD makes it hard to choose what to pay attention to at any given moment. And it can explain why people with ADHD might be so absorbed in something that they don't notice their name being called loudly.

Chapter 8: Inner Space and Being of An ADHD

What Is ADHD? Spiritual Causes And Roots Of ADHD

What is ADHD? In simple terms, attention deficit hyperactive disorder is a condition that combines the inability to maintain focus, hyperactivity that's extremely wearing, and an impulsive desire to interrupt frequently.

It affects children and teenagers but can also appear and continue in adulthood. In children, problems with inattention can result in poor performance, but these issues aren't due to lack of understanding or defiance – these characteristics often indicate the early presentation of ADHD.

One of the conflicts concerning ADHD diagnosis is whether it is a disorder or natural behavior that is misunderstood and unacceptable according to social norms. To understand this, we will first look at how ADHD is diagnosed and later discuss other perspectives and ways to overcome this syndrome.

The Probable Causes of ADHD

What causes ADHD remains unclear. Preliminary research has led to inconclusive assumptions that may include:

1. **Issues During Development:** Where problems in the central nervous system at key stages may be a reason
2. **Genetics:** Studies indicate that genes may play a role as the condition often runs in families
3. **Premature Birth:** And low birth weight may be a link
4. **Environmental Influences:** Lead exposure as a child has been cited as a possible cause

Learn To Prioritize

The ability to prioritize and manage thoughts and actions is crucial to life. Difficulties completing tasks or forgetting important things causes problems in every area of work. Treatment involves helping deal with the emotional and behavioral response to situations. Learning effective coping strategies is helpful to plan for organization and prioritization. Goal-setting, reward and consequence, and emotional regulation are other areas addressed during psychotherapy for ADHD.

Concentration Issues

The symptoms of inattention and concentration difficulties include:

- Being easily distracted by noises, activity, or other external events that others tend to ignore.
- Difficulty paying attention or focusing, such as when reading or listening to others.

- "Zoning out" without realizing it, even in the middle of a conversation.
- Struggling to complete tasks, even ones that seem simple. A tendency to overlook details, leading to errors or incomplete work.
- Poor listening skills, for example, having a hard time remembering conversations and following directions.

Disorganization And Forgetfulness

- Poor organizational skills
- Tendency to procrastinate
- Trouble starting and finishing projects
- Chronic lateness
- Frequently forgetting appointments, commitments, deadlines
- Constantly losing or misplacing things (keys, wallet, phone, documents, bills).
- Underestimating the time it will take you to complete tasks.

Impulsivity

- Frequently interrupt others or talk over them
- Poor self-control, addictive tendencies
- Blurting out thoughts that are rude or inappropriate without thinking

- Acting recklessly or spontaneously without regard for consequences
- Trouble behaving in socially appropriate ways (such as sitting still during a long meeting)

Emotional Difficulties

- Easily flustered and stressed out
- Irritability or short, often explosive, temper
- Low self-esteem and sense of insecurity or underachievement
- Trouble staying motivated
- Hypersensitivity to criticism
- Hyperactivity or Restlessness
- Feelings of inner restlessness, agitation, racing thoughts
- Getting bored easily, craving for excitement, tendency to take risks
- Talking excessively, doing a million things at once
- Trouble sitting still, constant fidgeting

A Different Perspective On ADHD

Many of the symptoms listed in the ADHD diagnosis list may well be considered as normal behavior in many cultures. This kind of behavior may also result from several factors, including neglect and lack of ways for children to express their creative energy. The harsh societal conditions that limit children's potential and behavior have been linked to several developmental conditions that include ADHD.

Perhaps, one of the ways of looking at ADHD is that children and adults are not in the right space and framework to connect with themselves and express their true nature. Seeing ADHD from this spiritual perspective, we can say that blocking this energy of the individual's essence may result in cognitive disorders and symptoms listed above.

If the root cause of ADHD is spiritual, then a different route could be followed to bring back a sense of balance to people suffering from this disorder. If you believe that there's a spiritual reason behind ADHD, then this aspect should be explored.

Spiritual causes and roots of ADHD may be directly related to the absence of awareness of our deeper spiritual connection. This is not simply about a specific religion or system of belief. It goes beyond to have a connection with your inner self or higher self. The question arises, is ADHD a mental disorder, or is it a lack of connection with our essence/spirit / true self?

The medication also questions whether people living with ADHD are being taken away from their true selves when non-medical options are available. Up-to-date research shows that diet has a direct relation to the disorder, a healthy eating regime with lesser sugar and processed food can help reduce several symptoms.

Adjusting Emotions Through Spiritual Guidance

When a person's essence within is fully alive, it changes brain function to learn acceptable behavior. A living, personal spirit allows the individual to learn what expressions are appropriate under normal conditions. When we can be fully comfortable with this true sense of self, we no longer need to act out and create situations that cause trouble to ourselves or others.

It also provides rest and solace so that other functions can happen. This includes learning in a school or college environment and the development of intellect. Combine this with learning from mistakes and integrating the complete function of spirit, body, mind, and soul into a balanced person, and you have stability, manners, and respect without assistance.

The Benefits Of Ayahuasca For People With ADHD

Visiting an ayahuasca retreat, like Spirit Vine center in Brazil, is a safe way to have a deep, guided journey into the spiritual side of life with the help of ayahuasca. Every part of the retreat is designed to help you achieve a state of harmony and develop a deeper connection with your essence. The workshops during the retreat are a space to learn techniques that can be applied during the ayahuasca ceremony and everyday life to keep the same level of connection gained during the retreat. The program includes time to integrate your experiences with guidance – and there's also plenty of time to relax and reflect.

You'll need to prepare for the ayahuasca retreat by stopping any medication three months before your stay. About two months before, you'll need to adjust your diet by moving to vegetarian or vegan options. Eating processed and packaged foods aren't recommended – freshly prepared organic foods help detoxify the body, which will put you in the space to get the most out of your ayahuasca retreat. You'll be able to get much more preparation details from the Spirit Vine website.

An ayahuasca experience in the proper setting is both sacred and profound. Ceremonies take place during the darkness of night, with music playing that helps bring awareness of the root causes of blockages and disorders to the surface. And according to current research, ayahuasca may protect brain cells and stimulate neural cell growth.

Helping to find the source of depression and addiction disorders, boosting mood, and improving mindfulness are other important key factors resulting from a well-done ayahuasca retreat. The key is to dedicate the proper time and preparation for the retreat, as it can be an intense process. There's a wealth of evidence suggesting people make changes to their lives after drinking ayahuasca as a single retreat can bring a sense of transformation that's very real.

This spiritual journey is certainly a path for people with ADHD interested in personal growth and spirituality. Ayahuasca may offer real benefits where spiritual growth and a connection to something greater than one's self can be fostered.

The Inner Workings Of ADHD Minds

There is a consensus that mornings are evil, or at least there should be. You're groggy, maybe you didn't get enough sleep, and the cruel world has yanked you from paradise. Most mornings, I disagree with the urgency of my alarm clock. "Do I need an hour before I leave the house? I can make it to class in 30 minutes, so 30 minutes it is."

But I do need that hour, if not more. ADHD dulls your sense of urgency. I'll take a shower, make breakfast, eat, get dressed. So far, I'm on track, but then I remember that there's a long gap between my classes, and I'd like to listen to music. Where are my earphones? They're in a drawer with an assortment of random stuff. No, not that drawer, the other one. While I'm at it, let me find my spare car key. Also, I haven't seen my Swiss Army knife in a while. Maybe I should look for it. And just like that, my preemptive strike at not being late to class is sabotaged by inattention and impulse.

ADHD is an acronym that stands for Attention Deficit Hyperactive Disorder. As the name suggests, ADHD is when a person exhibits inattention and hyperactivity. Another symptom that isn't in the name is impulsivity.

Now, you may have already encountered a person with the condition, or you might have it yourself. The chances are that if you don't have it, you're misinformed about its symptoms. ADHD people are not ballistic ricocheting cannonballs of pure energy as they are sometimes depicted on television. I am nowhere near hyperactive (unless I decide to drink coffee. If I do, buckle up, people!).

People with ADHD have varying symptoms. There are three different types of ADHD. ADHD-PI means that a person is 'primarily Inattentive' A primarily inattentive person most likely finds it hard to organize, keep time, remember details and retain focus through long tasks. They may lose things, forget appointments, and become distracted quickly. ADHD-PH/I means that a person is 'Primarily Hyperactive/Impulsive.' A primarily hyperactive/impulsive person may fidget excessively, interrupt others in conversations and activities, blurt out answers out of turn or when not being spoken to, talk excessively, and move excessively in inappropriate situations. ADHD-C means that a person has 'combined' symptoms; they exhibit both hyperactive/impulsive symptoms, along with inattentiveness. My diagnosis is ADHD-PI. But what racked my brain more than the diagnosis was how I had gotten ADHD in the first place.

In searching for the triggers of ADHD in the brain, research has found that the brains of subjects with ADHD matured later in their childhood. Furthermore, they produced smaller quantities of two hormones than a neurotypical person: dopamine and norepinephrine. Dopamine assists in movement, memory, learning, reward, behavior, cognition, attention, sleep, and mood. A brain deficient in dopamine may experience inattention, behavioral problems, mood problems, and learning impediments. Also, since dopamine is responsible for pleasure, a person who lacks dopamine can be severely under-stimulated while performing tasks like homework and may opt to procrastinate.

Despite all the information I've learned about the condition, ADHD is still tricky for me. As far as I can remember, I've always hated sitting in one place for way too long. As a kindergartener, I would cry to no end when I had to write sentence after sentence to improve my handwriting. In elementary school, I'd find out about homework only when the teacher would say it was time to turn it in. In middle school, achieving an A grade was the golden dream, locked away in a treasure chest, far out of reach for my mental capacity. In high school, I developed a system called W.O.A.H.: Work Only After Hyperventilating. Whenever I received an assignment, the task sheet got shoved to the bottom of my bag. The night before the assignment, I'd find the sheet. I'd sweat and shake, and I'd Work Only After Hyperventilating. I'd show up to class with bloodshot eyes, but I didn't care as long as the grade was good. I rationalized that this method of working was completely normal and that I was just a lazy person. I had been told by almost all of my teachers that I was 'smart but lazy.' The smart part satisfied me, and after a while, I began to agree with laziness. This all stopped in university. After a few semesters of using WOAH, I realized that it wasn't practical to pull all-nighters most days of the week. I decided to kick my 'lazy' habits and become responsible.

I couldn't.

I began by trying to start homework as soon as it was assigned. I attempted to finish my readings a whole day before they were due. I tried to spend every moment of class time paying attention. What ended up happening? I slept in class more often, and boredom eventually won over all my attempts. I would get fed up with work so quickly that sometimes the deadline would come and pass, and I wouldn't care. I knew I had a problem. I was sure I was putting in A-grade effort into my work, but the result was a plummeting GPA. I would look around at my peers who made succeeding look so easy while trying to swim through concrete. I was embarrassed and ashamed of myself. I began to harbor very negative thoughts about myself. I became anxious, emotional, and easily overwhelmed. When I finally tried to find help, I was diagnosed with mild anxiety along with severe ADHD-PI. I was prescribed medicine that worked until it didn't. I had read forums of people who had taken ADHD medicine that had turned their lives 180 degrees. But mine was flipped an entire 360 but with added potholes. I was suffering side effects with no benefits.

The road to diagnosis also wasn't a simple one. At first, I was thought to have anxiety and depression. I explained to the doctor that this is a cyclical thing for me. First, it starts with inattentiveness: I fail to perform well, which leads to an anxiousness surrounding academic work. If I remain anxious for a long time, I lose motivation and no longer want to do anything, hence, depression. The doctor did not listen to what I had to say and prescribed me antidepressants.

I tend to imagine depression and anxiety as a frequency chart with peaks and troughs. The lows signal depressive episodes, and the peaks signal anxious episodes. Both depression and anxiety would have an erratic chart with high peaks and low troughs that contrast greatly. An antidepressant would decrease the amplitude of these to those who don't have depression and anxiety. Since my depression and anxiety were contingent and not inherent, the antidepressant smoothed out even my normal peaks and troughs. I became numb, tired, and unresponsive to social settings. All I ever wanted to do was sleep.

After arguing with my doctor, he placed me on two other medicines to battle a depression that I did not have. The depression diagnosis never made sense to me as I was seeking help for my inattentiveness, and from my research, I most likely had ADHD. While I did follow my doctor's orders and took medicine, I had to take matters into my own hands eventually and see another doctor. After taking some tests and evaluations for ADHD, I was diagnosed with a severe case of ADHD-PI.

You might assume that this would have made me upset, but it didn't. It was a weight off my shoulders. The diagnosis explained so much of the anguish that had gone into my academic career. When I was prescribed medicine for ADHD, I thought I would climb to the very top of the academic ladder. Indeed, the first few weeks, the medicine worked like a charm. I would be on top of assignments from the moment they were assigned. I took notes like a stenographer. Aside from the dry mouth and cold hands side effects, I was on a roll. Over the weeks, however, the effectiveness wore off, and I started having bouts of rage. My temper was now shorter than my attention span. I then visited online forums about others with the same problem and learned that not everyone responds well to medication.

Treatment is not always a walk in the park. Whereas some people quickly determine the right treatment plan for themselves, others have a hard time. I stopped using ADHD medicine and decided to measure what exacerbated my symptoms and what calmed them. Nowadays, I focus mainly on behavioral changes. If I have too much sugar, my focus virtually disappears, and so does the daily routine that I built for myself. Not enough sleep does the same. ADHD sneaks up on you, so I'm trying to keep my scatterbrain alert. For adults with ADHD, it is recommended that they stick to routines, use lists as reminders, and keep notes in places that they can easily see, label everything, keep all of their belongings in a very accessible space.

If the symptoms sound familiar to you, do not hesitate to research. The internet offers a plethora of information, some of it reputable and some not. A quick trip to your university health and wellness counselor should be a priority, as they will help determine whether or not to investigate your concerns further. Lastly, you can take this test as a preliminary measure to determine whether you have ADHD symptoms or not.

Chapter 9: Guide For Parents To Treat Attention Deficit Hyperactivity Disorder

ADHD Parenting Tips

Does your child have attention deficit hyperactivity disorder? Learn what you can do to manage their behavior and deal with common ADHD challenges.

How To Help Your Child With ADHD

Life with a child or teen with attention deficit hyperactivity disorder (ADHD or ADD) can be frustrating, even overwhelming. But as a parent, you can help your child overcome daily challenges, channel their energy into positive arenas, and bring greater calm to your family. And the earlier and more consistently you address your child's problems, the greater chance they have for success in life.

Children with ADHD generally have deficits in executive function: the ability to think and plan, organize, control impulses, and complete tasks. That means you need to take over as the executive, providing extra guidance while your child gradually acquires executive skills of their own.

Although the symptoms of ADHD can be nothing short of exasperating, it's important to remember that the child who is ignoring, annoying, or embarrassing you is not acting willfully. Kids with ADHD want to sit quietly; they want to make their rooms tidy and organized; they want to do everything their parent says to do but they don't know how to make these things happen.

ADHD And Your Family

Before you can successfully parent a child with ADHD, it's essential to understand the impact of your child's symptoms on the family. Children with ADHD exhibit a slew of behaviors that can disrupt family life. They often don't "hear" parental instructions, so they don't obey them. They're disorganized and easily distracted, keeping other family members waiting. Or they start projects and forget to finish them, let alone clean up after them. Children with impulsivity issues often interrupt conversations, demand attention at inappropriate times, and speak before thinking, saying tactless or embarrassing things. It's often difficult to get them to bed and to sleep. Hyperactive children may tear around the house or even put themselves in physical danger.

Because of these behaviors, siblings of children with ADHD face several challenges. Their needs often get less attention than those of the child with ADHD. They may be rebuked more sharply when they err, and their successes may be less celebrated or taken for granted. They may be enlisted as assistant parents and blamed if the sibling with ADHD misbehaves under their supervision. As a result, siblings may find their love for a brother or sister with ADHD mixed with jealousy and resentment.

The demands of monitoring a child with ADHD can be physically and mentally exhausting. Your child's inability to "listen" can lead to frustration, and that frustration to anger followed by guilt about being angry at your child. Your child's behavior can make you anxious and stressed. If there's a basic difference between your personality and that of your child with ADHD, their behavior can be especially difficult to accept.

To meet the challenges of raising a child with ADHD, you must be able to master a combination of compassion and consistency. Living in a home that provides both love and structure is the best thing for a child or teenager to manage ADHD.

ADHD Parenting Tip 1: Stay Positive And Healthy Yourself

As a parent, you set the stage for your child's emotional and physical health. You have control over many of the factors that can positively influence your child's disorder's symptoms.

1. **Maintain A Positive Attitude:** Your best assets for helping your child meet the challenges of ADHD are your positive attitude and common sense. When you are calm and focused, you are more likely to connect with your child, helping him or her be calm and focused as well.

2. **Keep Things In Perspective:** Remember that your child's behavior is related to a disorder. Most of the time, it is not intentional. Hold on to your sense of humor. What's embarrassing today may be a funny family story ten years from now.

3. **Don't Sweat The Small Stuff And Be Willing To Make Some Compromises:** One chore left undone isn't a big deal when your child has completed two others plus the day's homework. If you are a perfectionist, you will be constantly dissatisfied and create impossible expectations for your child with ADHD.

4. **Believe In Your Child:** Think about or make a written list of everything positive, valuable, and unique about your child. Trust that your child can learn, change, mature, and succeed. Reaffirm this trust daily as you brush your teeth or make your coffee.

Self-Care

As your child's role model and most important source of strength, it is vital that you live a healthy life. If you are overtired or have simply run out of patience, you risk losing sight of the structure and support you have so carefully set up for your child with ADHD.

1. **Seek Support:** One of the most important things to remember in rearing a child with ADHD is that you don't have to do it alone. Talk to your child's doctors, therapists, and teachers. Join an organized support group for parents of children with ADHD. These groups offer a forum for giving and receiving advice and provide a safe place to vent feelings and share experiences.

2. **Take Breaks:** Friends and family can be wonderful about offering to babysit, but you may feel guilty about leaving your child or leaving the volunteer with a child with ADHD. Next time, accept their offer and discuss honestly how best to handle your child.

3. **Take Care Of Yourself:** Eat right, exercise, and find ways to reduce stress, whether taking a nightly bath or practicing morning meditation. If you do get sick, acknowledge it and get help.

Tip 2: Establish Structure And Stick To It

Children with ADHD are more likely to complete tasks when they occur in predictable patterns and predictable places. Your job is to create and sustain structure in your home so that your child knows what to expect and what they are expected to do.

Tips For Helping Your Child With ADHD Stay Focused And Organized:

1. **Follow A Routine:** It is important to set a time, and a place for everything to help the child with ADHD understand and meet expectations. Establish simple and predictable rituals for meals, homework, play, and bed. Have your child lay out clothes for the next morning before going to bed, and make sure whatever he or she needs to take to school is in a special place, ready to grab.

2. **Use Clocks And Timers:** Consider placing clocks throughout the house, with a big one in your child's bedroom. Allow enough time for what your child needs to do, such as homework or getting ready in the morning. Use a timer for homework or transitional times, such as between finishing up play and getting ready for bed.

3. **Simplify Your Child's Schedule:** It is good to avoid idle time, but a child with ADHD may become more distracted and "wound up" if there are many after-school activities. You may need to adjust to the child's after-school commitments based on the individual child's abilities and particular activities' demands.

4. **Create A quiet Place:** Make sure your child has a quiet, private space of their own. A porch or a bedroom works well, as long as it's not the same place as the child goes for a time-out.

5. **Do Your Best To Be Neat And Organized:** Set up your home in an organized way. Make sure your child knows that everything has its place. Lead by example with neatness and organization as much as possible.

Tip 3: Encourage Movement And Sleep

Children with ADHD often have the energy to burn. Organized sports and other physical activities can help them get their energy out in healthy ways and focus their attention on specific movements and skills. Physical activity benefits are endless: it improves concentration, decreases depression and anxiety, and promotes brain growth. Most importantly for children with attention deficits, however, exercise leads to better sleep, which can also reduce the symptoms of ADHD.

Find a sport that your child will enjoy and that suits their strengths. For example, sports such as softball that involve a lot of "downtime" are not the best fit for children with attention problems. Individual or team sports like basketball and hockey that require constant motion are better options. Children with ADHD may also benefit from training in martial arts (such as tae kwon do) or yoga, which enhance mental control as they work out the body.

ADHD And Sleep

Insufficient sleep can make anyone less attentive, but it can be highly detrimental for children with ADHD. Kids with ADHD need at least as much sleep as their unaffected peers but tend not to get what they need. Their attention problems can lead to overstimulation and trouble falling asleep. A consistent, early bedtime is the most helpful strategy to combat this problem, but it may not completely solve it.

Help your child get better rest by trying out one or more of the following strategies:

- Decrease television time and increase your child's activities and exercise levels during the day.
- Eliminate caffeine from your child's diet.
- Create a buffer time to lower down the activity level for an hour or so before bedtime. Find quieter activities such as coloring, reading, or playing quietly.

- Spend ten minutes cuddling with your child. This will build a sense of love and security as well as provide a time to calm down.
- Use lavender or other aromas in your child's room. The scent may help to calm your child.
- Use relaxation tapes as background noise for your child when falling asleep

Tip 4: Set Clear Expectations And Rules

Children with ADHD need consistent rules that they can understand and follow. Make the rules of behavior for the family simple and clear. Write down the rules and hang them up in a place where your child can easily read them.

Children with ADHD respond particularly well to organized systems of rewards and consequences. It's important to explain what will happen when the rules are obeyed and when they are broken. Finally, stick to your system: follow through each time with a reward or a consequence.

As you establish these consistent structures, keep in mind that children with ADHD often receive criticism. Be on the lookout for good behavior and praise it. Praise is especially important for children who have ADHD because they typically get so little of it. These children receive correction, remediation, and complaints about their behavior but little positive reinforcement.

A smile, positive comment, or another reward from you can improve your child's attention, concentration, and impulse control with ADHD. Do your best to give positive praise for appropriate behavior and task completion while giving as few negative responses as possible to inappropriate behavior or poor task performance. Reward your child for small achievements that you might take for granted in another child.

Tip 5: Help Your Child Eat Right

Diet is not a direct cause of attention deficit disorder, but food can and does affect your child's mental state, which in turn seems to affect behavior. Monitoring and modifying what, when, and how much your child eats can help decrease the symptoms of ADHD.

All children benefit from fresh foods, regular meal times, and staying away from junk food. These tenets are especially true for children with ADHD, whose impulsiveness and distractedness can lead to missed meals, disordered eating, and overeating.

Children with ADHD are notorious for not eating regularly. Without parental guidance, these children might not eat for hours and then binge on whatever is around. The result of this pattern can be devastating to the child's physical and emotional health.

Prevent unhealthy eating habits by scheduling regular nutritious meals or snacks for your child no more than three hours apart. Physically, a child with ADHD needs a regular intake of healthy food; mentally, mealtimes are a necessary break and a scheduled rhythm to the day.

- Get rid of the junk foods in your home.
- Put fatty and sugary foods off-limits when eating out.
- Turn off television shows riddled with junk-food ads.
- Give your child a daily vitamin-and-mineral supplement.

Tip 6: Teach Your Child How To Make Friends

Children with ADHD often have difficulty with simple social interactions. They may struggle with reading social cues, talk too much, interrupt frequently, or come off as aggressive or "too intense."

Their relative emotional immaturity can make them stand out among children their age and make them targets for unfriendly teasing.

Don't forget, though, that many kids with ADHD are exceptionally intelligent and creative and will eventually figure out for themselves how to get along with others and spot people who aren't appropriate as friends. Moreover, personality traits that might exasperate parents and teachers may come across to peers as funny and charming.

Helping A Child With ADHD Improve Social Skills

It's hard for children with ADHD to learn social skills and social rules. You can help your child with ADHD become a better listener, learn to read people's faces and body language, and interact more smoothly in groups.

- Speak gently but honestly with your child about their challenges and how to make changes.
- Role-play, various social scenarios with your child. Trade roles often and try to make it fun.
- Be careful to select playmates for your child with similar language and physical skills.
- Invite only one or two friends at a time at first. Watch them closely while they play and have a zero-tolerance policy for hitting, pushing, and yelling.
- Make time and space for your child to play, and reward good play behaviors often.

Best Activities For Kids With ADHD

Just like some activities will appeal more to other kids but may not necessarily appeal to all children, it's a great idea to give something a try with your child and not push it if he or she doesn't like it. It's worth revisiting the activity later on again as just like toys, some children will hate a toy initially and then find interest in it later on as they develop.

Outdoor Activities For ADHD Kids

Outdoor activities are fantastic for kids with ADHD because it gives them space, freedom and an opportunity to use all that energy.

1. Swimming: Michael Phelps, who has ADHD, is one of the most amazing swimmers of our time. Swimming was a great outlet for his energy and drive.

2. Playgrounds: The great thing about playgrounds is that they are easy to find and accessible at all times of the day. If your kid needs to burn off some energy, a playground will provide a combination of activities for him or her to do. Your child can choose to play alone or with others too.

3. Cycling: Cycling is another great activity that allows your child to be active as well as learn to focus. Unlike team sports, there are no real rules, and if you bring your child to a large park with safe pathways, your child won't have to wait for traffic lights to change or anything like that. There is enough changing scenery for your child to stay interested too.

4. Hiking: Hiking provides the opportunity to be in a peaceful environment and teach attention to details, such as looking at plants, flowers, and insects. There is also the freedom to go faster or slow down and explore different things along your hike.

5. Jogging Or Running: Similar to hiking, but you are going at a quicker pace and burning a lot more energy. It would be helpful if you are pretty fit yourself so that you can keep up!

Indoor Activities Outside The Home For ADHD Kids

6. Bounce Play Centers: Bounce play centers are normally paid indoor centers that provide several inflatable structures that are safe for children to jump on to their heart's content.

7. Trampoline Parks: Similar to bounce play centers but instead of inflatable structures, you will find tons of trampolines.

8. Drama Classes: There seem to be many famous ADHD adults in the entertainment industry, including Jim Carrey and Will Smith. Perhaps the creativity, enthusiasm, and energy that comes from having ADHD make them more interesting and appealing entertainers?

9. Singing And Dancing Classes: Like drama, there are singers with ADHD who are doing well in the entertainment industry, such as Justin Timberlake.

10. Sports: Many ADHD kids can excel in sports because of their drive and energy. Sports can be a great way to help your child increase their ability to build social skills, listen to instructions, or wait for turns. However, if your child is not yet ready for the leap into a team sport, you can choose other kinds of sports based on individual play, such as badminton, tennis, and squash.

Enjoy The Parenting Journey

As with most things in life, it's a matter of perspective on whether something is a curse or a blessing. Although it will be challenging for you as a parent, it may be a great blessing for your child to have ADHD. In any case, enjoy your parenting journey. Just like any other parent, you will have fantastic days and days where you wished you could just stay in bed.

Chapter 10: Emotional Development In Children

Emotional Development

Emotional development refers to the ability to recognize, express, and manage feelings at different stages of life and to have empathy for the feelings of others. The development of these emotions, which include both positive and negative emotions, is largely affected by relationships with parents, siblings, and peers.

Infants between the ages of six and ten weeks begin to show emotion with a social smile accompanied by actions and sounds representing pleasure. The social smile develops in response to caregivers' smiles and interactions. Around three to four months, infants begin to laugh, which demonstrates that they can recognize incongruity in actions that deviate from the norm. Laughter fosters reciprocal interactions with others, which promotes social development. From six to twelve months, infants can begin to express emotions, such as fear, disgust, anger, and sadness, which indicate to caregivers that they are experiencing discomfort or displeasure and need attention. Infants will respond to their emotions to the degree that their caregivers respond and then learn from their emotional facial cues.

During a child's second year, toddlers begin expressing shame, embarrassment, and pride, which are learned emotions based on their culture. As they acquire language and learn to verbalize their feelings, they can express their emotions of affection, distress, pain, and fatigue. The ability to recognize and label emotions and then control emotional expression in ways consistent with cultural expectations is called emotion regulation. Children learn to self-regulate their emotions to be able to cope with difficult situations. Usually, by age two, children also begin to acquire the complex emotional response of empathy by reading others' emotional cues and understanding their perspectives.

By the age of three, children understand society's rules regarding the appropriate expression of emotions. Caregivers teach them that expressions of anger and aggression are to be controlled in adults' presence. Still, they are less likely to suppress negative emotional behavior around their peers. This difference is the result of differing consequences of their behavior with adults or with peers.

Children acquire the ability to alter their emotional expressions by around age four. They can display external expressions that do not match their internal feelings, such as thanking a gift-giver when the gift is not liked. This ability requires complex skills of understanding the need to alter their expression, realizing the perception of another, knowing that their expression does not need to match their actual feelings, and having the motivation and control to mask their true feelings convincingly.

A wider variety of self-regulation skills is displayed by children ages seven to eleven. Factors that influence their emotion management decisions include the type of emotion experienced and the person's relationship, age, and gender. Children develop a set of expectations of the outcomes they will receive from different people. Parents might handle some emotions better than peers, who might be little or tease them.

As school-age children deal with their emotions and the people involved with them, they develop social skills. Based on how they perceive they compare with their peers, they either develop confidence and are competent in useful skills or feel inferior and unsuccessful. Their self-esteem is influenced by how they feel others view them. If their performance does not match their aspirations, they are likely to feel inferior and inadequate. Conditions that threaten to expose their inadequacies can cause anxiety. If children believe in themselves and their abilities, they can have a stable, positive self-concept about themselves.

During play, children increase their emotional maturity and social competence by interacting with other children. Play helps children practice their communication skills as they negotiate roles and appreciate others' feelings. They learn to share, wait their turn, and handle conflicts while playing with others. Play also allows children to express and cope with their feelings through pretend play, which allows them to think out loud about their experiences and feelings.

Emotional Development In Children And Emotional Competence

Emotional development includes an individual dimension, the ability to feel, express, and manage various emotions. It also includes a social dimension, the ability to recognize the presence of emotions in the other and understand them.

Emotional Development In Children

The theoretical perspective adopted concerning the child's emotional development combines functionalist theory and dynamic systems theory. A child's interactions with the environment can be seen as dynamic transactions that involve a multitude of emotional elements (e.g., expressive behavior, physiological structuring, action tendencies, goals and motivations, social and physical contexts, evaluations, and experiential feeling) that change over time, gradually as the child grows, and in response to environmental interactions.

Emotional development reflects social experience, including the cultural background. I have already argued that affective development should be viewed according to a bioecological framework in which human beings are considered dynamic systems rooted in a community context.

The Development Of Emotional Competence

A productive way of looking at emotional functioning is to see how well it serves the individual's accommodation and self-efficacy goals. The concept of emotional competence has been proposed to designate a set of affect-oriented behavioral, cognitive, and regulatory skills that appear over time as they grow up in a social context. Individual factors, such as cognitive development and temperament, do influence the development of emotional skills.

However, emotional competence skills are also influenced by previous social experiences and learning, including the person's relationship history and the belief and value system in which they live. Therefore, we actively create our emotional experience with the combined influence of our cognitive development structures and our social exposure to emotional discourse. Through this process, we learn what feeling emotions and reacting to them mean.

Here Are The Lists Of The Eight Skills Related To Emotional Competence:

- Awareness of your emotional development state, including the possibility of feeling many emotions and, at even higher levels of maturity, know that you may not realize that you have certain feelings because of unconscious dynamics or selective inattention.

- Ability to discern and understand others' emotions based on situational and expressive cues on which there is a certain level of consensus as to their emotional significance.
- Ability to use appropriate vocabulary to describe emotions and expressions in terms used in a person's subculture and, at higher levels of maturity, to acquire cultural scenarios related to emotions and social roles.
- Ability to show empathy and compassion towards others when they have emotional experiences.
- Ability to realize that the internal affective state does not need to correspond to the external expression, as much at home as in others and, at higher levels of maturity, ability to understand that one's emotional behavior and expressive can have an effect on others and take this fact into account when choosing self-presentation strategies.
- The ability to adapt to negative or distressing emotions through automated emotion strategies reduces these affective states' intensity or duration (e.g., stress resistance).
- Awareness that the structure or nature of relationships is partly defined by the degree of emotional closeness or sincerity in expressing emotions and the degree of reciprocity or symmetry within the relationship.

- Capacity for emotional self-efficacy. The individual considers that the way he feels overall is the way he wants to feel. Emotional self-efficacy, therefore, corresponds to the acceptance of the affective experience, whether unique and eccentric or culturally appropriate, and this acceptance is adapted to personal beliefs as to the definition of desirable affective "balance."

Social And Emotional Development In Early Childhood

A tremendous amount of social and emotional development takes place during early childhood. As kids experience temper tantrums, mood swings, and an expanding social world, they must learn more about their emotions and other people.

Social-Emotional Experiences Of Early Childhood

Throughout the toddler years, temper tantrums are quite common. There's a good reason why people often refer to this stage as the "terrible twos"!

Toddlers tend to have rapid mood swings. While their emotions can be very intense, these feelings also tend to be quite short-lived. You might be stunned at how your child can go from screaming hysterically about a toy at one moment to sitting in front of the television quietly watching a favorite show just moments later.

Children at this age can be very possessive and have difficulty sharing. Learning to get along with other children is an essential skill, however. In just a few short years, your child will go from spending most of their time with family and close friends to spending a large chunk of the day interacting, learning, and playing with other kids at school.

Emotional development and social skills are essential for school readiness. Examples of such abilities include paying attention to adult figures, transitioning easily from one activity to the next, and cooperating with other kids.

Help Kids Develop Social And Emotional Skills

So how can you help your child learn how to play well with others? Social competence not only involves the ability to cooperate with peers; it also includes such things as the ability to show empathy, express feelings, and share generously. Fortunately, there are plenty of things that you can do to help your kids develop these all-important social and emotional skills.

1. Model Appropriate Behaviors

Observation plays a vital role in how young children learn new things. If your child sees you sharing, expressing gratitude, being helpful, and sharing feelings, your child will have a good solid understanding of how to interact with other people outside the home. You can model these responses in your household with your child and other family members. Every time you say "please" or "thank you," you are demonstrating how you would like your children to behave.

2. Reinforce Good Behavior

Most importantly, be sure to offer praise when your children demonstrate good social behaviors. Helping your children feel good about themselves also plays an important role in developing a sense of empathy and emotional competence. By creating a positive climate where children can share their feelings, children will naturally begin to become more generous and thoughtful. Reinforcement makes young children feel good about themselves and helps them understand why certain behaviors are desirable and worthy of praise.

3. Teach Empathy

Parents can also boost empathy and build emotional intelligence by encouraging their children to think about others' feelings. Start by inquiring about your child's feelings, asking about events in your child's life. "How did you feel when you lost your toy?" "How did that story make you feel?"

Once children become skilled at expressing their emotional reactions, begin asking how other people may feel. "How do you think Nadia felt when you took away the toy she was playing with?"

By responding to questions about emotions, children can begin to think about how their actions might impact the emotions of those around them.

4. Teach Cooperation

Cooperation is one skill that benefits tremendously from direct experience. Giving your child the opportunity to interact and play with other kids is one of the best ways to teach them how to relate to others. While your toddler may find playing with peers frustrating at times, since kids often lack patience and the ability to share, things will gradually begin to improve with age and experience. As children play and interact, they also begin to develop social problem-solving skills.

Chapter 11 : Mood Foods: Holistic Eating For Managing ADHD

The Best And Worst Foods For ADHD

Attention-deficit hyperactivity disorder (ADHD) is a condition that affects both children and adults, although it is most commonly diagnosed in younger people. ADHD causes a variety of symptoms that can interfere with schoolwork, careers, and relationships. This condition affects everyone differently, but some of the most common symptoms of ADHD may include:

- Finding it hard to concentrate on one task for a long period
- Changing activities or tasks frequently
- Difficulty organizing time and tasks
- Fidgeting or difficulty sitting still
- Impulsive or aggressive behavior

ADHD is usually treated with medication, and some people with ADHD find therapies such as cognitive-behavioral therapy (CBT) helpful. Many people also find that diet plays an important role in managing the symptoms of ADHD. So what are the best and worst foods for ADHD? Let's take a closer look:

1. Protein

Protein is one of the most important nutrients for anybody with ADHD for two reasons.

Firstly, protein helps keep your blood sugar stable, meaning you are less likely to get spikes and crashes. Blood sugar crashes cause grogginess and makes it more difficult to concentrate, which you will want to avoid!

Secondly, protein is necessary for your body to produce neurotransmitters such as serotonin, noradrenaline, and dopamine. These chemicals play an important role in your mood and behavior, and keeping them in balance is crucial for anyone with ADHD. Some foods which are high in protein include:

- Meat
- Poultry
- Fish
- Eggs
- Dairy products
- Beans and pulses
- Nuts

As a general guideline, children should be eating around 24 grams of protein each day. Women should aim to eat 45 grams of protein daily, and men should aim to eat 55 grams.

It is especially important to eat some protein at breakfast time to ensure that you are set up well for the day. Try scrambled eggs or baked beans on wholegrain toast or muesli with fruit and yogurt.

2. Whole Grains

Like protein, whole grains provide you with a steady energy supply and help prevent sugar crashes. They also contain essential vitamins, minerals, and fiber which is necessary for healthy digestion. Some examples of whole grains include:

- Whole oats
- Brown rice
- Wholegrain barley
- Buckwheat
- Quinoa

It is easy to incorporate more whole grains into your diet by switching white rice for brown and white bread or pasta for wholemeal versions. You could also try adding barley to soups and stews or using buckwheat or quinoa as a base for salads.

3. Omega-3 Fatty Acids

Omega-3 fatty acids are a source of "good fats" necessary for healthy brain and nervous system function. There is plenty of research on omega-3 fatty acids for ADHD out there, and the evidence seems very positive. The best dietary sources of omega-3 fatty acids are oily, cold-water fish such as:

- Salmon
- Mackerel
- Sardines

A word of caution, though: Some scientists have suggested that eating fish containing high mercury levels could harm ADHD symptoms. Therefore, it is best to avoid larger fish like tuna, swordfish, or king mackerel.

4. Vitamin B6

Getting enough vitamin B6 is important as this micronutrient has a positive effect on the neurotransmitter dopamine. This could help to increase alertness and improve attentiveness in people with ADHD. Foods that are high in vitamin B6 include:

- Pork
- Poultry
- Fish
- Eggs
- Whole grains
- Fortified breakfast cereals
- Soy products
- Peanuts

The recommended daily intake of vitamin B6 is between 0.7 milligrams and 1.5 milligrams for children (depending on age and sex), 1.2 milligrams for women, and 1.4 milligrams.

5. Essential Minerals

Everybody needs enough vitamins and minerals in their diet, but this could be especially important if you have ADHD. Three of the most critical minerals for people living with ADHD are zinc, iron, and magnesium.

6. Zinc

Zinc influences dopamine action and may help improve the way that the drug methylphenidate (Ritalin) works. It can be found in meat, shellfish, dairy products, and cereals. Children should consume between 5 milligrams and 9.5 milligrams of zinc every day, women should consume 7mg, and men should aim for 9.5 milligrams.

7. Iron

Iron plays a role in the production of dopamine and is necessary for healthy red blood cells. Good sources of iron include meat, beans, nuts, and leafy greens. Children need between 6.9 milligrams and 14.8 milligrams of iron daily. Men of all ages and women over 50 need around 8.7 milligrams each day, but women of childbearing age require more at 14.8 milligrams daily.

8. Magnesium

Magnesium plays an important role in energy production and helps to regulate hormones and neurotransmitters. It can be found in meat, fish, nuts, leafy greens, dairy products, and brown rice. The recommended daily intake of magnesium is between 85 milligrams and 300 milligrams for children, 270 milligrams for women, and 300 milligrams for men.

Foods To Avoid If You Have ADHD

To determine whether a particular food is affecting you, you could try an elimination diet for a few weeks. This involves cutting out all foods you suspect could make things worse and eating as plain a diet as possible for two to three weeks. Then try reintroducing foods one by one and see how these affect you. It is a good idea to speak to a dietician before ensuring that you are not missing out on any essential nutrients.

Foods To Limit Or Avoid

Adults and children with ADHD may feel better if they limit or avoid the following:

1. **Sugar**

Eating sugary foods can cause blood glucose spikes and crashes, which can affect energy levels. Some caregivers report a link between sugar consumption and hyperactivity in children with ADHD. Simultaneously, some studies indicate a link between high sugar consumption and soft drinks with a higher prevalence of ADHD diagnosis. Even if it does not improve ADHD symptoms, limiting sugar intake is a healthful choice for everyone, as it may reduce the risk of diabetes, obesity, and tooth decay.

2. Other Simple Carbohydrates

Sugar is a simple or refined carbohydrate. Other simple carbohydrates can also contribute to rapid blood sugar levels, and people should only consume them in moderation. The foods below contain simple carbohydrates:

- Candy
- White bread
- White rice
- White pasta
- Potatoes without skins
- Chips
- Sodas
- Sports drinks
- Potato fries
- Caffeine

Small amounts of caffeine may benefit some people with ADHD. Some research suggests that it can increase concentration levels. However, caffeine can intensify the effects of certain ADHD medications, including any adverse reactions that a person may experience. Adults with ADHD should limit their caffeine intake, especially if they are taking ADHD medications. Children and teenagers should avoid tea, coffee, and cola completely.

3. Artificial Additives

Some children with ADHD can benefit from removing artificial additives from their diets. The American Academy of Pediatrics (AAP) recommends that children avoid these additives, particularly food colorings because they can worsen ADHD symptoms. Artificial additives may also interfere with hormones, growth, and development. Many prepackaged and processed products contain artificial coloring, flavors, and preservatives, including some:

- Breakfast cereals
- Candies
- Cookies
- Soft drinks
- Fruit punches
- Vitamins for children
- Allergens

Some researchers claim that removing potential allergens such as gluten, wheat, and soy can improve focus and reduce hyperactivity. However, eliminating these allergens likely only benefits those who have an allergy or intolerance. Consider discussing food allergies with a doctor or dietician before removing these foods from the diet.

Chapter 12: Build Self-Esteem

Having healthy self-esteem can influence your motivation, your mental well-being, and your overall quality of life. However, having self-esteem that is either too high or too low can be problematic. Better understanding your unique level of self-esteem can help you strike a balance that is just right for you. Self-esteem is a driving force behind our confidence and how we see and feel about ourselves. It encompasses our sense of value, significance, and self-worth. That's why learning how to build self-esteem is essential to personal growth and happiness.

A deep feeling of self-esteem is something that needs to grow and be nurtured over time. In this article, I will show you what you can do right now to improve your self-esteem. Then, you will realize your hidden potential and your self-worth.

What Is Self-Esteem?

In psychology, self-esteem is used to describe a person's overall subjective sense of personal worth or value. In other words, self-esteem may be defined as how much you appreciate and like yourself regardless of the circumstances. Many factors, including: define your self-esteem

- Self-confidence

- Feeling of security
- Identity
- Sense of belonging
- Feeling of competence

Other terms that are often used interchangeably with self-esteem include self-worth, self-regard, and self-respect. On the other hand, self-confidence is more about how you feel about your abilities and will vary from situation to situation. You can have great self-esteem (feeling good about yourself overall) but low self-confidence about a particular situation or event (e.g., public speaking). Or, maybe you've got great self-confidence in an area (e.g., a sport that you play) but low self-esteem overall.

A strong and solid sense of self-esteem comes from deep within, from a belief in your importance, your value, and your worthiness. The good news is that there are many ways to improve self-esteem, which we will look at below.

Why Self-Esteem Is Important

Self-esteem impacts your decision-making process, your relationships, your emotional health, and your overall well-being. It also influences motivation, as people with a healthy, positive view of themselves understand their potential and may feel inspired to take on new challenges. People with healthy self-esteem:

- Have a firm understanding of their skills

- Can maintain healthy relationships with others because they have a healthy relationship with themselves
- Have realistic and appropriate expectations of themselves and their abilities
- Understand their needs and can express them

People with low self-esteem tend to feel less sure of their abilities and may doubt their decision-making process. They may not feel motivated to try novel things because they don't believe they can reach their goals. Those with low self-esteem may have issues with relationships and expressing their needs.

People with overly high self-esteem may overestimate their skills and may feel entitled to succeed, even without the abilities to back up their belief in themselves. They may struggle with relationship issues and block themselves from self-improvement because they are so fixated on seeing themselves as perfect.

Factors That Affect Self-Esteem

Many factors can influence self-esteem. Your self-esteem may be impacted by:

- Age
- Disability
- Genetics
- Illness
- Physical abilities

- Socioeconomic status
- Thought patterns

Racism and discrimination have also been shown to have negative effects on self-esteem. Additionally, genetic factors that help shape a person's personality can play a role, but life experiences are the most important factor.

Healthy Self-Esteem

There are some simple ways to tell if you have healthy self-esteem. You probably have healthy self-esteem if you:

- Avoid dwelling on past negative experiences
- Believe you are equal to everyone else, no better and no worse
- Express your needs
- Feel confident
- Have a positive outlook on life
- Say no when you want to

Having healthy self-esteem can help motivate you to reach your goals because you can navigate life knowing that you can accomplish what you set your mind to. Additionally, when you have healthy self-esteem, you can set appropriate boundaries in relationships and maintain a healthy relationship with yourself and others.

Low Self-Esteem

Low self-esteem may manifest in a variety of ways. If you have low self-esteem:

- You may believe that others are better than you.
- You may find expressing your needs difficult.
- You may focus on your weaknesses.
- You may frequently experience fear, self-doubt, and worry.
- You may have a negative outlook on life and feel a lack of control.4
- You may have an intense fear of failure.
- You may have trouble accepting positive feedback.
- You may have trouble saying no and setting boundaries.
- You may put other people's needs before your own.
- You may struggle with confidence.

Low self-esteem can lead to a variety of mental health disorders, including anxiety disorders and depressive disorders. You may also find it difficult to pursue your goals and maintain healthy relationships. Having low self-esteem can seriously impact your quality of life and increases your risk of experiencing suicidal thoughts.

Excessive Self-Esteem

Overly high self-esteem is often mislabeled as narcissism. However, some distinct traits differentiate these terms. Individuals with narcissistic traits may appear to have high self-esteem, but their self-esteem may be high or low and is unstable, constantly shifting depending on the given situation. Those with excessive self-esteem:

- Maybe preoccupied with being perfect
- May focus on always being right
- May believe they cannot fail
- May believe they are more skilled or better than others
- May express grandiose ideas
- May grossly overestimate their skills and abilities

How To Improve Self-Esteem

Fortunately, there are steps that you can take to address problems with self-esteem. Some actions that you can take to help improve your self-esteem include:

1. Become More Aware Of Negative Thoughts: Learn to identify the distorted thoughts that are impacting your self-worth.

2. Challenge Negative Thinking Patterns: When you find yourself engaging in negative thinking, try countering those thoughts with more realistic and positive ones.

3. Use Positive Self-Talk: Practice reciting positive affirmations to yourself.

4. Practice Self-Compassion: Practice forgiving yourself for past mistakes and move forward by accepting all parts of yourself.

Low self-esteem can contribute to or be a symptom of mental health disorders, including anxiety and depression. Consider speaking with a doctor or therapist about available treatment options, which may include psychotherapy, medications, or a combination of both.

Ways To Build Lasting Self-Esteem

Many of us recognize the value of improving our feelings of self-worth. When our self-esteem is higher, we not only feel better about ourselves, we are more resilient as well. Brain scan studies demonstrate that when our self-esteem is higher, we will likely experience common emotional wounds such as rejection and failure as less painful and bounce back from them more quickly. When our self-esteem is higher, we are also less vulnerable to anxiety; we release less cortisol into our bloodstream when under stress, and it is less likely to linger in our system.

But as wonderful as it is to have higher self-esteem, it turns out that improving it is no easy task. Despite the endless array of articles, programs, and products promising to enhance our self-esteem, the reality is that many of them do not work, and some are even likely to make us feel worse.

Part of the problem is that our self-esteem is rather unstable, to begin with, as it can fluctuate daily, if not hourly. Further complicating matters, our self-esteem comprises our global feelings about ourselves and how we feel about ourselves in our lives' specific domains (e.g., as a father, a nurse, an athlete, etc.). The more meaningful a specific domain of self-esteem, the greater its impact on our global self-esteem. Having someone wince when they taste the not-so-delicious dinner you prepared will hurt a chef's self-esteem much more than someone for whom cooking is not a significant aspect of their identity.

Lastly, having high self-esteem is indeed a good thing, but only in moderation. Very high self-esteem like that of narcissists is often quite brittle. Such people might feel great about themselves much of the time. Still, they also tend to be extremely vulnerable to criticism and negative feedback and respond to it in ways that stunt their psychological self-growth.

That said, it is certainly possible to improve our self-esteem if we go about it the right way. Here are five ways to nourish your self-esteem when it is low:

1. Use Positive Affirmations Correctly

Positive affirmations such as "I am going to be a great success!" are extremely popular, but they have one critical problem they tend to make people with low self-worth feel worse about themselves. Why? Because when our self-esteem is low, such declarations are simply too contrary to our existing beliefs. Ironically, positive affirmations do work for one subset of people those whose self-esteem is already high. For affirmations to work when your self-esteem is lagging, tweak them to make them more believable. For example, change "I'm going to be a great success!" to "I'm going to persevere until I succeed!"

2. Identify Your Competencies And Develop Them

Self-esteem is built by demonstrating real ability and achievement in areas of our lives that matter to us. If you pride yourself on being a good cook, throw more dinner parties. If you're a good runner, sign up for races and train for them. In short, figure out your core competencies and find opportunities and careers that accentuate them.

3. Learn To Accept Compliments

One of the trickiest aspects of improving self-esteem is that when we feel bad about ourselves, we tend to be more resistant to compliments even though that is when we most need them. So, set yourself the goal to tolerate compliments when you receive them, even if they make you uncomfortable (and they will). The best way to avoid the reflexive reactions of batting away compliments is to prepare simple set responses and train yourself to use them automatically whenever you get good feedback (e.g., "Thank you" or "How kind of you to say"). In time, the impulse to deny or rebuff compliments will fade which will also be a nice indication your self-esteem is getting stronger.

4. Eliminate Self-Criticism And Introduce Self-Compassion

Unfortunately, when our self-esteem is low, we are likely to damage it even further by being self-critical. Since our goal is to enhance our self-esteem, we need to substitute self-criticism (which is almost always entirely useless, even if it feels compelling) with self-compassion. Specifically, whenever your self-critical inner monologue kicks in, ask yourself what you would say to a dear friend if they were in your situation (we tend to be much more compassionate to friends than we are to ourselves). Direct those comments to yourself. Doing so will avoid damaging your self-esteem further with critical thoughts and help build it up instead.

5. Affirm Your Real Worth

The following exercise has been demonstrated to help revive your self-esteem after it sustained a blow: Make a list of qualities you have that are meaningful in the specific context. For example, if you got rejected by your date, list qualities that make you a good relationship prospect (for example, being loyal or emotionally available); if you failed to get a work promotion, list qualities that make you a valuable employee (you have a strong work ethic or are responsible). Then choose one of the items on your list and write a brief essay (one to two paragraphs) about why the quality is valuable and likely to be appreciated by other people in the future. Do the exercise every day for a week or whenever you need a self-esteem boost.

The bottom line is improving self-esteem requires a bit of work, as it involves developing and maintaining healthier emotional habits but doing so, and especially doing so correctly, will provide a great emotional and psychological return on your investment.

Ways To Build More Self-Esteem In Your Child

Healthy self-esteem is one of the most important characteristics of healthy child development. A child's social, behavioral, and emotional health will play a crucial role in handling setbacks, peer pressure, and other challenges throughout life. Positive self-esteem is also a protective factor for good mental health. Cultivating confidence contributes to positive social behavior and works as a buffer when negative situations impact your child.

1. Know What Healthy Self-Esteem Looks Like

Self-esteem is basically how children see themselves including what they think of themselves and their ability to do things. It's also shaped by how much they feel loved and how much support and encouragement (or criticism) they receive from important people in their life, like their parents and their teachers. Meanwhile, being self-confident does not mean thinking that the world revolves around you or that your needs are more important than those of other people. Likewise, healthy self-esteem is not arrogance, narcissism, or entitlement. Balance out your child's self-esteem with other important life skills such as having empathy, being kind, having good manners, being charitable, and having a sense of gratitude.

2. Show Unconditional Love Every Day

Knowing how much you love them gives your children a sense of security and belonging crucial to their view of themselves. Your unconditional love lays the groundwork for all the healthy and strong relationships they will form later in their lives. So hug your kids when you say goodbye, snuggle together and read a book, and express your love every single day. As your kids grow, this foundation of love will help them as they continue to build their social circles, make friends, and form bonds with teammates.

3. Play Together And Have Fun

When you play with your child, it shows them that you like spending time with them and values their company. Just having fun with your child has numerous benefits for both of you. Not only do kids develop confidence in their ability to be an interesting and entertaining person who can form solid social bonds, but studies have shown a child's odds of being happy increases, and their risk of depression and anxiety decreases when kids engage in healthy play.

4. Give Your Child Responsibilities And Chores

Being responsible for doing age-appropriate chores gives your child a sense of purpose and accomplishment. Even if they don't do something perfectly, let them know that you appreciate their efforts. Praise them for all the things they do well and reassure them that they'll get better and better at many things, including their chores over time. Having chores and responsibilities also gives kids a sense of control over their lives. And in a time when things are unpredictable, having responsibility for small jobs around the house can go a long way in building confidence and resilience.

5. Encourage Independence

The elementary school years are a time of fast-growing independence in kids. By the time they reach the middle-school years, many children start to spend time alone at home, walking to school by themselves, and helping younger siblings. It would help if you allowed your kids to grow them increasingly figure out how to talk to teachers about any problems on their own, organizing assignments, making sure their soccer uniforms are packed and ready, and so on. So-called helicopter parenting undermines kids' abilities to do things on their own and negatively impacts their self-esteem. It also robs them of autonomy.

6. Refrain From Insulting Your Child

When your child does something that drives you crazy or misbehaves, be sure to separate the behavior from your child. You're human when your child pushes your buttons, you'll probably be irritated or even angry. Experiencing these feelings is completely normal, but don't engage in name-calling or shame your child. Instead, talk to your child with respect. Don't yell. Take the emotion out of your discipline. A good way to do this is by using natural and logical consequences and speaking to your child in a pleasant and friendly tone.

7. Make Setbacks Learning Experiences

Emphasize the fact that being human means making mistakes and not being perfect. Teach your child to view setbacks as opportunities for improvement and growth. Be patient with your child when they make mistakes. If you find that they tend to act out at school or experience behavior problems, do what you can to turn those situations into growth opportunities. Doing so will help build your child's confidence and demonstrate that making mistakes is not the end of the world as long as they address it healthily.

8. Let Them Create And Show Off Work

Let your child display their work around the house. When they create artwork, write a story, or put together a school project, invite your child to tell you about their work. Ask what they want people to think or feel and what they like best about their creations.

Giving children a chance to show off what they make or talk about the things they create lets them know that their hard work is worthy of attention. It also communicates that their opinions and thoughts matter.

How To Build Self-Esteem? Ways To Boost Your Self-Esteem

1. Identify The Triggers That Lower Your Self-Esteem

If you are looking for ways to build self-esteem, you need to identify the triggers that make you unhappy. Take a look at yourself and try to find the root cause of low self-esteem. It can be related either to your personal or professional world. Take a long look at the cause and contemplate your next course of action. If it is possible to remove it from your vicinity, do so, and if you cannot change it, then accept it and let it go. Once you start dealing with your unhappiness, you are opening yourself to replace it with joy and positivity. Remember, it is your happiness that will build self-esteem to reach your goals in life.

2. Set Realistic Expectations

One of the main reasons for low self-esteem is unrealistic expectations from yourself. Yes. It is good to have dreams in your life, but it is more important to set realistic goals to fulfill those dreams properly and timely.

3. Comparisons Are Never Good Enough

You cannot judge yourself every time you contact someone you find charismatic and powerful if you are looking for ways to build self-esteem. Human beings are social animals, and you need to have direct and indirect contact with others regularly. We come across several goods at different things, and it is natural if you are in awe of such talent. That does not give you the license to start making illogical comparisons between you two. Remember, you pity your weaknesses against some other person's strengths by identifying and comparing your weak points and your strong ones. Appreciate the qualities of people you come in contact with and consider this opportunity as a learning curve to develop your skills, talent, and education. Just change your perspective and relax your mind, and you will find the emotional and mental balance necessary to build self-esteem.

4. Know Your Worth

Know your worth and be glad about your skills, knowledge, and behavior if you are looking for ways to build self-esteem. Your inner self will help you in valuing your qualities and abilities so that you can appreciate them. Take charge of your actions and perceive the actual power you have over yourself.

5. Stop Considering Others Smarter Than You

Humans tend to become insecure about both relevant and irrelevant things at the drop of a hat. If you contact someone more skillful, powerful, wealthy, or even smarter, then your insecurities flare-up. It is a natural reaction, and you need to take viable steps to curb it effectively.

6. Use Your Vulnerabilities For Your Benefit

Do you feel vulnerable in new settings or when you come across people that you consider more talented and efficient than yourself? Does your brain disregard your strengths and start harping on your weaknesses. Change your demeanor and mindset and try to find your balance so that the pressure and misery do not wreak havoc in your life.

7. Stop Worrying About Others

A person is responsible only for his actions and not about the acts of others. You cannot determine your worth by the actions of others. Suppose in a social setting someone has snubbed you and was bitching about your appearance, then do you lower your value because another person has judged you harshly.

If you do so, then remember you are doing yourself wrong because others do not have the right to become your judge and jury as the privilege rests in your hands only. If you are looking for ways to build self-esteem, then stop thinking about the opinions of others.

8. Replace Perfection With Accomplishments

If you wait to create something perfect, I am sorry to say that you will be waiting for a long time. Perfection is overrated; hence opt for accomplishments if you are looking for ways to build self-esteem. Accept that you are never going to achieve a perfect job, perfect relationship, or perfect surroundings. Think about what you have accomplished to date and be happy and proud of your achievements because these feelings will help build and boost your confidence and self-esteem.

9. Be Decisive And Take Viable Action

Be decisive and take viable action if you are looking for ways to build self-esteem. You have identified your thought patterns, and now is the time to take action to remove any negative emotions from your surroundings.

Remember, self-esteem is built through your decisive actions, and it is not dependent on the actual outcome of your action. Hence, train yourself to stop being vulnerable to situations or other people and gain the confidence to move forward irrespective of prevalent conditions.

10. Find Your Balance

If you are looking for ways to build self-esteem, then you need to address your inner critic as soon as possible. Identify the negative emotions swirling inside your head and deal with them by replacing negative thoughts with positive ones.

Let go of anger and despair and integrate self-worth and joy in yourself. Start by putting your needs at the forefront and giving yourself the importance you deserve. Remember, there is no need to prove your value to others. It is enough that you recognize and acknowledge them as an integral part of yourself. This acceptance will ultimately help you find the right balance between your emotional, physical and mental well-being.

11. Create Your Happiness

Happiness can only be felt when you are happy from within. You do not have to search for it from outside sources. Think about your accomplishments and how every achievement has taken you one step forward towards your goals.

Recognize that you deserve the opportunities coming your way and accept that you deserve to be happy. Believe in your worth and be proud if you are looking for ways to build self-esteem. Your hard work and determination have helped you reach higher levels of success in life.

12. Choose A Healthy Diet

Scientists worldwide think that the stomach has a direct link with the brain because when it is satiated, our brain also relaxes and when it feels hunger pangs, the muscles in the brain also go in overdrive. It is important to take great care of the food you are feeding to the stomach as it may impact the mental frame of a person.

Eat a balanced and nutritious diet that will result in a healthy lifestyle and a positive mental frame. The healthy nutrients of fresh fruits and green vegetables increase a person's productivity and boost his energy levels. Choosing a healthy and balanced diet is a great way to build self-esteem and increase an individual's well-being.

13. Replace Self-Criticism With Self-Appreciation

One of the main reasons for low self-esteem is the ability to criticize yourself unnecessarily. Do not cast doubts on your abilities and aspirations; instead, replace them with positive thoughts and affirmations? Remember, self-doubts are damaging and can result in serious repercussions.

Stay away from them if you are looking for ways to build self-esteem. Make sure to identify the areas where you are competent and start highlighting your achievements. Learn to accept and give genuine compliments as it will boost your emotional balance as well as self-esteem. Affirm your actual worth through self-appreciation because until and unless you recognize it, no one else will do for you.

14. Practice Meditation And Start Exercises

One of the best ways to relax your body and mind is by participating in physical exercises and deep breathing via meditation. You need to find a quiet corner for meditation, place your mat, and sit with your legs folded in the correct posture. Breathe in and out at a regular rhythm and let go of every negative thought from your mind. It is time to let yourself fly freely through positive surroundings. Exercises also help individuals let go of excess energy from their bodies to find the right balance between emotional and mental states. Practice meditation and exercises if you are looking for ways to build self-esteem.

15. Choose Healthy Connections

Choose healthy connections in your life if you are looking for ways to build self-esteem. No need to maintain relationships where you will have to prove yourself regularly. Stay away from toxic people who spread negativity in their surroundings.

Remember, only one bad fish can make the pond dirty, and similarly, one rotten personality can create low conditions. Surround yourself with optimistic people who have a healthy and positive mindset towards life in general, as their positive approach will be reflected in your abilities and traits. Be happy when you see others in a joyful mood because a viable shift in mindset will bring forth desired success and joy in your own life.

16. Keep A Journal

If you are looking for ways to build self-esteem, then you need to maintain a journal. Write down your positive as well as negative thoughts in it. Remember, once you jot down your thoughts, it loses the actual impact. Read them after some time and try to find the cause of your unhappiness.

Self-esteem is all about appreciating yourself despite any perceived weaknesses or strengths. It makes us more content and resilient because a person has now gained the necessary confidence to tackle and balance his emotional and mental strength. Failure and rejection do not hurt as much as before and instead become a stepping stone on the path of progress. The vulnerability minimizes as the confidence level increases in an individual. Once you have built your self-esteem, you start recognizing your worth, and this emotional wellbeing ultimately culminates into personal happiness and joy in life.

Conclusion

Getting a diagnosis of ADHD may not be the most welcome news, but the good thing is that now you have an explanation for the challenges you and your child have faced. Additionally, being aware of what has been causing the inattention, trouble focusing, and inability to sit still makes it easier for you both to address these issues more effectively. Before you know it, things will begin improving in your child's academic and social life.

Please find out how your child understands his behavior. Attempt to understand his behavior and the challenges he faces in light of his executive functioning deficits. It is extremely important to see your child through a strengths-based lens and focus on enhancing those strengths

Talk to your child about what he perceives as his strengths and give your view on his strengths. Use a notebook to write down what you like about your child, what he does well (include special talents, interests, and hobbies). Brainstorm together with your child what he can work toward enhancing these.

Whether medical, psychological, or sociological, new ways of living with the condition are constantly being tested. There is more social acceptance of ADHD than ever before, and support for parents and other caregivers increases. Life may need more planning and thought with a child who has ADHD. It can, however, be just as pleasurable and fulfilling.

A successful school strategy for a child with ADHD must meet the triad of academic instruction, behavioral interventions, and classroom accommodations. While the regular implementation of these strategies can make a world of difference to a child with ADHD, they will also benefit the whole classroom environment. ADHD can be dealing with boredom particularly difficult, but finding ways to cope with dull moments can help. Being prepared can be one of the best tools for coping with boredom.

When you have ADHD, keeping your attention on a task often means that it needs to be something you are interested in, that you want, or find challenging. When boredom hits, turning to an activity you enjoy or presenting a challenge can help give your brain the stimulation you need. Always consult your doctor before making any changes to your treatment. They need to be aware of every supplement and medication you're taking to be alert for potential interactions or problems with other conditions you may have.

Parenting a child with ADHD can be challenging but is not impossible. Practicing healthy habits like exercising regularly, eating a balanced diet, and getting enough sleep is also important for managing symptoms of ADHD. If you suspect you or your child is exhibiting the condition's symptoms, you should see a medical expert as soon as you can for a proper diagnosis and treatment plan.

Don't feel rushed to make decisions about treatment; allow yourself a little time to process the new information before moving on to the next steps. Once you're ready, you can meet with your doctor to determine what treatment course is best for you, including therapy, medication, and lifestyle changes.

Your treatment plan should be customized to fit your needs and your lifestyle. It's important to monitor your symptoms and your progress to continue finding the strategies and treatments that help you live well with ADHD.

Although there isn't a cure for ADHD, the symptoms can usually be well-managed. Your child's symptoms are also likely to change with age, which is normal. Your child's treatment will likely need to be adjusted over time, however, so it's important to continue monitoring symptoms and progress. Although raising a child with ADHD poses some extra challenges, with support and appropriate interventions, kids with ADHD can thrive.

If your child has recently become a target of bullying, it's never too late to help them develop stronger social and emotional skills. Over time, if you work on their social and friendship-making skills and teaching assertiveness, and instilling self-esteem, they will feel more confident in dealing with difficult situations, including bullying. Plus, these are important life skills that will benefit them for the rest of their lives. Living well with ADHD is about monitoring your symptoms and actively working toward finding what works best for you. With the right support and treatment, you can create a life that allows you to reach your greatest potential.

The journey to higher self-esteem will be challenging, but the challenge builds depth, strength, character, and resilience. If the reward is greater self-esteem, which leads to greater relationships, a better career, increased health and well-being, more success, and a greater sense of self-worth, it's worth it.

While you live in a society where you are constantly bombarded with messages of not being enough and how you could be better, remember this:

- You are deserving of love, happiness, and success. You are imperfectly perfect. It's not by chance that you have arrived here, on this planet, at this very time, and even if you feel inadequate, unlovable, or unworthy, know that you are none of those things.
- You may not be able to believe this yet, but some part of you, deep down inside, knows this to be true.

Now, it's time to take the steps above and realize it for yourself.

Though some of the causes of low self-esteem can't be changed, such as genetic factors, early childhood experiences, and personality traits, there are steps you can take to feel more secure and valued. Remember that no one person is less worthy than the next. Keeping this in mind may help you maintain a healthy sense Sof self-esteem.

Made in United States
North Haven, CT
25 May 2022

19536684R00137